INSIGHTS INTO
MODERN HINDUISM

INSIGHTS INTO MODERN HINDUISM

By

HERVEY DE WITT GRISWOLD

GYAN

Published by

GYAN

Gyan Publishing House
5, Ansari Road
Daryaganj, New Delhi-110002
Phone: 011-47034999, 9811692060
E-mail: books@gyanbooks.com

Distribution Network
gyanbooks.com
India, USA, Canada, UK, Australia, France

ISBN : 978-81-212-9779-0 (PB)
First Published, 1934

2nd Impression 2023

Printed at: Gyan Press, Delhi.

INSIGHTS INTO MODERN HINDUISM
Author: HERVEY DE WITT GRISWOLD

STUDIES IN RELIGION AND CULTURE

SCHERMERHORN LECTURES II

INSIGHTS INTO MODERN HINDUISM

INSIGHTS INTO MODERN HINDUISM

BY

HERVEY DE WITT GRISWOLD

DEDICATED (WITH PERMISSION) TO

DR. RUDOLF OTTO

Professor of Theology

Marburg University, Germany

PREFACE

LIKE every other living religion contemporary Hinduism presents a multitude of varying aspects. One might go on endlessly dealing with this and that facet of its many-sided structure. During my sojourn of over thirty years in India, much of the time on the staff of the Forman Christian College, Lahore, I became interested in the study of religious movements and prepared a number of monographs, some of which were used by the late Dr. J. N. Farquhar as source material for his book, *Modern Religious Movements in India.* This study was continued in 1928 and 1929 at Columbia University, where as visiting professor I lectured on Hinduism.

Hinduism in India like the Roman form of Christianity in Europe may be called "catholic." Both have been all-inclusive for many centuries. Then came the revival of learning, the European in the fifteenth century, the Indian in the nineteenth, followed in each case by religious reformation. In both Europe and India movements of "protest" against the dominant "catholic" form of religion broke out, the reformed sects of India—Brahmo Samaj, Arya Samaj, etc.—corresponding to the Protestant churches of the West. Hence to determine the inner genius and spirit of Hinduism it is necessary to deal not only with orthodox and catholic forms, but also with the various protesting and schismatic forms, including also the religion of the outcastes. Hinduism is also face to face with the aggressive religions, Islam and Christianity, the reactions ranging all the way from stern opposition to downright acceptance, as in the case of Pandita Ramabai and Sadhu Sundar Singh, whose Christianity is fragrant with the aroma of the choicest things of Hinduism.

An attempt has been made to maintain a reasonably objective attitude, with what success the reader must judge.

I am grateful to Professors Schneider and Friess of Columbia University for many helpful suggestions.

I thankfully acknowledge permission to quote from material issued by the following publishers:

THE MACMILLAN COMPANY

1. *Brahman: A Study in the History of Indian Philosophy,* by H. D. Griswold, 1900.
2. *Modern Religious Movements in India,* by J. N. Farquhar, 1915.
3. *The Coming Religion,* by Nathaniel Schmidt, 1930.
4. *Mahatma Gandhi's Ideas,* by C. F. Andrews, 1930.
5. *Encyclopædia of the Social Sciences,* Art. Brahmanism and Hinduism, by H. D. Griswold, 1930.
6. *The Religion of Man,* by Rabindranath Tagore, 1931.

THE UNIVERSITY OF CHICAGO PRESS

The Biblical World, Sept. 1912, pp. 163-172.

THE BEACON PRESS

Hinduism Invades America, 1930. Permission received from Wendell Thomas, the author, who holds the copyright.

My thanks are also due to the following publishers:

CHARLES SCRIBNER'S SONS, publishers of the American edition of *The Encyclopædia of Religion and Ethics.*

OXFORD UNIVERSITY PRESS

1. *Indian Theism,* by Nicol Macnicol, 1915.
2. *The Heart of Jainism,* by Mrs. Sinclair Stevenson, 1915.
3. *An Outline of the Religious Literature of India,* by J. N. Farquhar, 1920.
4. *Religion of the Rigveda,* by H. D. Griswold, 1923.
5. *Indian Islam,* by M. T. Titus, 1929.

I must plead guilty to some inconsistency in spelling. Sometimes a word appears in two forms, e.g., Vivekananda (Skt. form) and Vivekanand (Hindi form). The pronunciation is practically the same.

H. D. G.

20 Rowsley St., Bridgeport, Conn.
March 1934

CONTENTS

INSIGHTS INTO MODERN HINDUISM

CHAPTER I

INTRODUCTORY

1. RELIGIOUS SIGNIFICANCE OF INDIA IN THE HISTORY OF THE WORLD

THE term "Hinduism" may be used to designate the form of religion dominant in India throughout the three thousand years of the historical period. In this large sense Hinduism has been a great force in the world's history. During most of the Christian era that form of Hinduism which proved historically best fitted for export, namely Buddhism, has powerfully influenced the whole Mongolian world, leaving its impress upon nearly one-third of the human race. It is a paradoxical fact that, while India's linguistic and ethnological connections are largely with the West, its religious conquests have been in the East. For the supreme achievement of Hinduism was the Buddhist penetration of the Mongolian world. Besides the major racial, religious, and cultural contacts of Dravidian and Aryan, Hindu and Muhammadan, Indian and European, which have taken place on the soil of India, there have been numerous minor but fruitful contacts, such as the very early commercial relations with the Semitic world, as proved by the

Brahmi and Kharoshthi scripts, the various tribal invasions from Central Asia, the contact with Greece through Alexander and his successors, the diplomatic and commercial contact with the Roman Empire, and the Indian migrations and settlements in Cambodia and Java. Notwithstanding these contacts India enjoyed up to the time of the Islamic penetration a comparative isolation which made possible an independent religious development.

There are on earth only two birthplaces or creative centers of the world's great religions, namely Palestine-Arabia and India-Persia. And two races alone have been religiously creative, the Semitic race, producing Hebraism, Christianity, and Muhammadanism, and the Aryan race, producing Hinduism, Zoroastrianism, and Buddhism. These six highly developed religions are all found in the Indian Empire, and their statistics according to the census reports of 1901, 1911 and 1921 are as follows:

	1901	*1911*	*1921*
1. Aryan religions			
a. Hinduism	207,147,026	217,504,557	216,734,586
b. Buddhism	9,476,759	10,000,000	11,571,268
c. Zoroastrianism	94,190	100,000	101,778
2. Semitic religions			
a. Muhammadanism	62,458,077	68,000,000	68,735,233
b. Christianity	2,923,241	3,876,000	4,753,174
c. Judaism	18,228	21,000	22,000

Thus it will be seen at a glance that the Indian Empire is remarkable for being not only a birthplace of religions, but also in modern times a sphere of competition for all the major faiths of the world. For example, in most non-Christian countries the chief rival of Christianity is either Buddhism alone or Islam alone, but in the Indian Empire Christianity is confronted at once by Hinduism, Islam, and Buddhism, the three strongest non-Christian religions.

It may not be without interest in this connection for people of the West to remind themselves that they are largely Aryan, at least in language and probably in blood as well, and that though they are now Semitic in religion, yet originally they were Aryan in this also, the original religion of most of them being Teutonic, Celtic, Slavonic, Roman, or Greek. The primitive Aryan religions of Europe have all been superseded by religions of Semitic origin, but in Asia Aryan religion still exists in full vigor. And India, as the home of Hinduism and the birthplace of Buddhism, has this permanent interest for all whose general connection is Aryan, that whatever of religious creativeness slumbered in the Aryan race, in India and Persia alone came to full and abiding fruition. While the religions of Aryan Europe all fell before the triumphant march of Semitism, the Aryan religions of India and Persia still influence the life of nearly one-third of the human race. Of the three great religious penetrations of history, two consist of the Semitic penetration of Europe and the two Americas through Christianity and the Semitic penetration and conquest of the Nearer East through Islam. The third is constituted by the Aryan penetration of the Farther East through Buddhism.

2. HINDUISM AS CONDITIONED BY THE CLIMATE OF INDIA

India lies between latitude 8° and 38° north and longitude 66° and 96° east. The greatest length and breadth are about the same, 1,800 or 1,900 miles. The plains of the Ganges and the Indus river systems are only a few hundred feet above the sea, and are shut in on the north by the chain of the Himalayas and on the south by the Vindhyas and the Rajputana desert. The result is that the great northern plain of India extending from Eastern Bengal to the Indus is for six or eight months of the year one of the hottest places on the face of the earth. The effect of such a climate may be summed up by saying that it is against activity. Some religious, theological, and eschatological implications may be mentioned.

A. *India is the home of meditation.* The climate predisposes to a meditative calm. The most typical religious attitude is that of the Buddha or of some ascetic or holy man of Hinduism sitting engaged in profound thought. Such a scene furnishes one of the most characteristic pictures of Indian life. According to Hinduism it is also the attitude of the ripest religious attainment. A Sannyasi holds himself absolved from all ordinary rites and ceremonies, but not from the meditative life. Meditation is a mystical exercise and is indicative in itself of the large mystical element in Hinduism. Probably one good influence of Hinduism over other religions will be to encourage the use of silence and meditation in worship.

Hence the Christian Church, which is being raised up on the soil of India, may well become rich in meditation as well as in activity.

B. In the philosophically most impressive type of Hinduism *Ultimate Reality is conceived as static,* not dynamic, as the changeless *Brahman* over against the changeful *Maya.* This way of conceiving ultimate reality is quite in accordance with the dislike of activity which is such a prominent result of the heat of India. One who has lived in India, or visited India, knows well the leisurely way in which all work is done. According to the *advaita* philosophy of India there are two, and only two, fundamental categories, the changeless and the changeful, the inactive and the active, *Brahman* and *Maya.* Brahman is described as *sat,* "reality," *chit,* "intelligence" and *ananda,* "bliss." The intellectual and the emotional are here covered, but not the volitional and active. The human preference in the intense heat of India for the static and the inactive is carried back into the conception of Ultimate Reality.

C. Quite in harmony with the static conception of Ultimate Reality, as the theological or philosophical implication of the dislike of activity, is *the eschatological implication.* The goal of hope is release from the changeful *Maya,* the sphere of transmigration, and absorption into, or recognition of identity with, the Ultimate Reality, where there is infinite and changeless calm. It is true, there are other eschatological views held in India, but transmigration and the hope of "release" are the most common. Final bliss is often pictured as a *dreamless sleep,* in which the dualism of subject and object is obliterated. This is regarded as the very image of *reality.* The blessedness of the future life is ever conceived in terms of that which is most delightful in this life. Such is the experience of sleep in the hot climate of India.

D. The Indian climate is probably one cause at least of *Indian pessimism.* We all know how differently a bracing day and a sultry day affect the mood. The first exhilarates and creates a mental atmosphere in which pessimistic thoughts do not thrive. Whereas the intense heat of the long hot season, followed by the rainy season with its damp and muggy weather, harder to bear than the dry heat, and the illnesses which succeed the rains, malaria, etc., and the filthy unpleasantness of numerous dust storms, all combine to create a mood favorable to pessimism. One cannot say that the Indian climate alone has created Indian pessimism. But this much can be said, that the Indian climate at its worst engenders a mood for which a pessimistic outlook constitutes the line of least resistance. Whether this line will be taken depends in its turn on the view of life which is held. Given a climate which makes life a burden for six or eight months in the year, and a metaphysical view which postulates an indefinitely large number of rebirths, presumably in the same climatic area, and one cannot wonder that pessimism is the result.

E. The climate of India has been against the assertion of *personality,* for personality is never more real than in moments of fundamental choice. But in choice and decision one is active. The philosophical and theological reverberation of the *negative attitude toward human personality* is seen in the doctrine of the impersonal *brahman.*

F. The climate of India calls for *biological modification and adjustment,* if newly introduced types of life coming from colder regions are to live and thrive. For example, there is a poultry business at Etah in the United Provinces, India. It was found that pure-blooded varieties from colder countries would not thrive in India except by crossing with a suitable Indian breed. The same thing holds true of humanity. It was not only historically inevitable, but also biologically necessary that there should be, to a greater or less degree, a fusion of the invading Aryans and the indigenous Dravidians. Only thus could the Aryans become really acclimated.

3. HINDUISM AS CONDITIONED BY THE ISOLATION OF INDIA

The supremely important invasions of India have been four: Dravidian, Aryan, Muslim, and European. Between the Aryan invasion (B.C. 2000-1500) and the Muslim invasion (C. 1000 A.D.) some two or three thousand years intervened. During this period there were numerous minor invasions of Persians, Greeks, Scythians, Parthians, Kushans, and Huns, which modified the ethnology of the western half of India, but did not seriously disrupt India's customs. Hence India during this period experienced a *relative isolation* from the rest of the world, and the result of it was negatively the absence of disintegrating forces from the outside, and positively the undisturbed working out of a national religion and culture, and the maintenance intact of certain customs which had come down as "archaic survivals" [1] from the Indo-European period. Shilotri in his dissertation, *Indo-Aryan Thought and Culture,* remarks: "This fact of isolation has played the most prominent rôle in sealing the fate of the Indo-Aryan civilization." Hence was born "that rigid attitude of the Indian social mind," which supports "the tyranny of the Brahmanical law and institutions." And Prof. MacDonell writes: "The importance of ancient Indian literature as a whole largely consists in its originality. Naturally isolated by its gigantic mountain barrier on the north, the Indian peninsula has ever since the Aryan invasion formed a world apart over which a unique form of Aryan civilization rapidly spread, and has ever since prevailed. When the Greeks, towards the end of the fourth century B.C., invaded the north-west, the Indians had already fully worked out a national culture of their own, unaffected by foreign influences. And, in spite of successive waves of invasion and conquest by Persians, Greeks, Scythians, Muhammadans, the national development of the life

[1] *Religion of the Rigveda* by H. D. Griswold, p. 20.

and literature of the Indo-Aryan race remained practically unchecked and unmodified from without down to the era of British occupation. No other branch of the Indo-European stock has experienced an isolated evolution like this."[2]

4. THE INDIGENOUS DEVELOPMENT OF HINDUISM

As pointed out above, the independent religious development of India is the result, in large part, of its *isolation.* Hence from the Vedic period down to the present time there has been a continuous evolution which in its most important features may be traced. "If Vedism represents a polytheism of nature gods and Brahmanism in its deepest insight the doctrine of a single spiritual reality, then Hinduism (in the narrower sense) furnishes a kind of synthesis of the two, namely, a revised polytheism grounded in the pantheistic one and all."[3] These three periods represent respectively, "the way of *works,*" "the way of *knowledge,*" and "the way of *devotion,*" a kind of Hegelian thesis, antithesis, and synthesis. The tendency of Upanishad speculation was to resolve the multiplicity of the Vedic nature gods into the unity of Absolute Being. "So radical is the Indian doctrine of immanence that the whole universe is regarded as an incarnation of God, and hence everything in

[2] *History of Sanskrit Literature,* p. 7.

[3] Art. *Brahmanism and Hinduism* by H. D. Griswold, in *Encyclopædia of the Social Sciences,* Vol. II, p. 676. By permission of the Macmillan Company, publishers.

heaven, on earth and under the earth may be worshipped—333,000,000 gods," a god for every man, woman and child in India—while at the same time the claim is made, according to the Upanishad point of view, that God is one.* Such is the main line of orthodox Hindu development.

Now comes a very significant contrast. The course of India's religious and cultural development has never been broken, at least not between 1500 B.C. and 1000 A.D., whereas the course of the parallel Aryan development in Europe was cut through by the penetration of Christianity and the passing of the ancient Aryan cults. The people of Europe and of the two Americas are Christian, that is to say Semitic, in religion, but in customs and institutions, social and political, they are largely Aryan. This involves a kind of dualism in loyalty, which does not exist in India. There everything is the fruit of the Aryo-Dravidian development—religion, language, art, literature, social organization, philosophy; and in all of these notable achievements the Hindus are proud of their past and loyal to it. For them the secular past is also the religious past. For the Aryans of the West, however, the religious element has one source and the secular another. The result is that in the West one becomes a Christian from conviction, not from motives of patriotism and loyalty to the past; whereas in India patriotic reverence and loyalty are strong forces in support of traditional religion.

* *Ibid.*

5. DEFINITIONS OF HINDUISM

There are two types of definition, the first explaining Hinduism as a system of religion, and the second dealing with it as an anthropological process. It goes without saying that the first point of view is that of conservative Hinduism, and of those Western scholars who base their findings upon the Hindu religious literature. The orthodox view is that a man to be a Hindu must ordinarily be born a Hindu and must conform to the ways of Hinduism. Sir Alfred Lyall emphasizes birth: "Hinduism is a matter of birthright and inheritance. . . . A man does not become a Hindu, but is born into Hinduism."[4] In another passage, however, the same author defines Hinduism in terms of conformity as "the collection of rites, worships, beliefs, traditions, and mythologies that are sanctioned by the sacred books and ordinances of the Brahmans." Dr. J. N. Farquhar also stresses conformity. A man is a Hindu because of two things, birth and conformity, the latter applying to four groups of actions:

(a) marriage, food, occupation, residence;
(b) domestic ceremonies;
(c) ancestor worship; and
(d) worship of the gods.[5]

[4] Too strong a statement. Not to mention the reception into Hinduism of Nancy Miller, wife of the ex-Maharaja of Indore, Hinduism has always been a missionary religion in the sense that it is constantly receiving aboriginal tribes into its fold as separate castes.

[5] *Primer of Hinduism*, 2nd Ed., 1912, pp. 177-181.

In reply to the question, "Who is a Hindu?" R. B. Shrisha Chandra Vidyarnava [6] answers, "He who accepts the Vedas, the Smritis, the Puranas and the Tantras as the basis of religion, and the rule of conduct, and believes in one supreme God (Brahm), in the law of Retributive Justice (Karma) and in Reincarnation (punarjanma)." Here the emphasis is on doctrinal conformity. Guru Parsad Sen defines Hinduism in terms of conduct as the doing of "what the Hindus or the major portion of them in a Hindu community do." [7] Note the emphasis on social and ethical conformity.

According to the second type of definition Hinduism is a growth or process. This is the point of view of the modernist. Hinduism, says Govinda Das, is "an anthropological process, to which, by an irony of fate, the name of 'religion' has been given." [8] The same view is taken by Sridhar V. Ketkar: [9] "There is no 'Hindu religion.' Hinduism, which means the Hindu society and its traditions, is not a religion, but is akin to tribal or national culture;" and again, "Present Hinduism is nothing but a mixture of heterogeneous tribes and their traditions."

Here Govinda Das, late member of the Court, Council and Senate of the Benares Hindu University and Sridhar V. Ketkar, who received the doctorate from Cornell University in 1910, both agree that

[6] *A Catechism of Hindu Dharma*, 1919.
[7] *Census of India*, I, 356.
[8] *Hinduism*, p. 45.
[9] *Essay on Hinduism*, pp. xxiv and 26.

Hinduism is primarily not a religion, but a cultural or anthropological process, having many aspects—social, political, industrial, artistic, literary, etc.—only one of which is religious.

Govinda Das goes on further to say: Hinduism "rejects nothing. It is all-comprehensive, all-absorbing, all-tolerant, all-complacent, all-compliant. . . . It may in the future enwrap within its tenuous folds even such aggressive religions as Christianity and Islam." The same modernist Hindu scholar defines both negatively and positively what constitutes a Hindu. ✓Neither Hindu birth nor Hindu conformity is necessary, in order to be a Hindu. One may be born anywhere, of any parents, may disbelieve in God, the Vedas, the Caste system, the sanctity of the cow and of Brahmans, the Hindu sacraments and rules, Karma, re-incarnation, and all the rest, and yet may be rightfully called a Hindu, provided that, (1) he "does not repudiate that designation, or better still, because more positive, . . . says he is a Hindu, and (2) accepts any of the many beliefs and follows any of the many practices that are anywhere regarded as Hindu."[10] It may be noticed that, while transmigration, Karma, and Caste, constitute the creed and practice of the ordinary conservative Hindu, a modernist, like Govinda Das, reduces all that is distinctive in Hindu doctrine and conduct to the vanishing point. Apparently he was not so much interested in main-

[10] *Hinduism*, pp. 45, 50-57.

taining Hinduism as a religion as he was in its preservation as a cultural type.

Somewhat similar to the view of Govinda Das is that of R. E. Hume, who describes Hinduism as "the complex gradual growth of a very religiously minded people with many different temperaments." [11] Thus Hinduism, if not a religion, at least has its origin in "a very religiously minded people." As a spontaneous growth Hinduism is to some extent distinguished from the instituted religions, Zoroastrianism, Buddhism, Christianity, and Muhammadanism, which go back to great creative personalities.

A spontaneous growth, however, is sure to include heterogeneous elements, such as the popular and the philosophic. Says Sir Charles Eliot: "Hinduism is an unusual combination of animism and pantheism, which are commonly regarded as the extremes of savage and philosophic belief." [12] Much the same is Risley's characterization of Hinduism as "Animism more or less transformed by philosophy, or magic tempered by metaphysics." These two definitions emphasize the synthetic character of Hinduism as the home at once of animism and philosophy, magic and metaphysics, and as the medium for the resolution of their inner contradictions.

[11] *World's Living Religions,* p. 19.
[12] *Hinduism and Buddhism,* Vol. I, p. 5.

CHAPTER II

CHARACTERISTICS OF HINDUISM AS A RELIGION[1]

A. HINDUISM has always had the general animistic or pantheistic *tendency to deify whatever is.* This tendency may be illustrated from every period of its history. In the Rigveda, the earliest literary monument of Hinduism, divine honor is paid to heaven and earth, sun, wind, fire, dawn, rivers, mountains, trees, sacrificial implements, the cow, dead ancestors, etc., "gods many and lords many," worshipped singly or in combination. The test for the selection of objects of worship was a pragmatic one. Whatever force or object of nature was useful to man or striking in appearance or effects was a candidate for apotheosis. Just as in the Roman Church there are conditions which must be fulfilled before sainthood can be recognized, so in the Vedic age there were pragmatic tests which had to be satisfied before godhood could be acknowledged. Take for example Agni, the Vedic fire-god. The uses of fire are manifold. It banishes darkness, dispels the goblins of the night, and frightens away enemies. It is the secret of vegetation and

[1] Reprinted by permission from the *Biblical World,* Sept. 1912, pp. 163-172, University of Chicago Press.

of the growth of food. As heat it has to do with generation and life. Fire serves as a means for cooking, and in its character as fire on the altar it was the center of the Vedic ritual. Given an animistic or pantheistic attitude toward nature, the apotheosis of nature is almost inevitable. The points of view which led to such apotheosis are presented with striking fulness and detail in the Agni hymns of the Rigveda. By the pragmatic test of usefulness or striking appearance such physical phenomena as the thunderbolt, the rain-cloud, fire, sun, wind, soma, dawn, received deification.

Now the Vedic attitude has been the general point of view of Hinduism throughout its whole history. The Vedic presuppositions and the Vedic methods of apotheosis have been determinative and prophetic. Some years ago an orthodox Brahman in Kashmir indicated that he regarded everything in nature, down to separate stick and stone and blade of grass, as possessed each by its own spirit. "Otherwise, how could it exist at all?" he asked. This view of the Kashmiri Pandit reveals a fundamental characteristic of Hinduism, namely, a *radical* doctrine of the immanence of God. If the Christian believes that "God was in Christ reconciling the world unto himself" (2 Cor. 5 : 19) and accordingly worships Christ as *the* incarnation of God, the Hindu believes that God is in sun, moon, wind, and thunderbolt, in cow, monkey, and serpent; in the *pipal* tree and the *tulsi* plant, in Ram and Krishna, and he accordingly worships any or all of these as manifestations of God. The underlying presupposition is the thoroughgoing immanence of God in nature. And since everything is a manifestation of the divine, it is left to the particular society or individual to select an *ishta devata,* or preferred god, each according to his own good pleasure. This thoroughgoing immanence is not to be construed as an equal immanence. Things differ in excellence—"one star differeth from another in glory," one animal from another animal, one tree from another tree, one man from another man. Such differences are correlated, presumably, with the amount of the divine essence present in the things compared. The better the object or personality, the more of the divine essence present. Hence the Hindu belief that God is present in a unique degree in the unique things of earth, e.g., the ice-*linga* of the Amar Nath Cave as compared with all other pieces of ice, in Sri Ram and Sri Krishna as contrasted with all other heroes, in the Brahman Caste in comparison with all other castes, and in the Hindu people as distinguished from all other peoples.

B. A second general characteristic of Hinduism is *the tendency to syncretism.*

This also is abundantly illustrated in the Rigveda. Hillebrandt well says, "Vedic mythology is not a system, but a conglomerate, a kind of mythological 'confusion of tongues,' which arose through the coming together and fusion of the traditions of different clans."[2] In all probability each separate Vedic clan had originally its own tribal god, or at least had a simpler pantheon than that provided by the Rigveda collection in its final form. There is a good deal of evidence for the belief that the hymns to the "all-gods" as well as many hymns to dual gods are the work of "mediatory theologians," as Hillebrandt calls them. Consider the parallel situation in Israel in the days of Solomon and Ahab. Israel had its own tribal god *Yahweh,* but on account of the foreign alliances, both political and matrimonial, of Solomon and Ahab, there was an incoming flood of religious syncretism, which threatened to destroy the old religious landmarks altogether. Yahweh was in danger of being placed on the same level as Baal and Ashtoreth of the Sidonians, Chemosh of the Moabites, and Milcom of the Ammonites. And in spite of the strong protest on the part of Elijah and other prophets, syncretism almost carried the day. In Vedic India there was no protest, so far as is known, against such a mediatory tendency. In fact, syncretism accords with the very genius of Hinduism. For example, in the *Indra-Agni* hymns of the Rigveda, Agni is assimilated to Indra and Indra to Agni. The *Bhagavadgita* is also a monument of religious syncretism. Buddha was taken into the Hindu system and made one of the incarnations of Vishnu. If everything alike is a manifestation of God according to the principle of radical immanence, then each people or tribe

[2] *Vedische Mythologie,* III, S. xii.

has a right to worship anything in heaven, on earth, or under the earth, according to its own sovereign taste and good pleasure. This helps to explain the boundless hospitality which Hinduism has always shown towards every conceivable form of religious belief and practice. For it, too, is missionary in its own way. It annexes not individuals as a rule but whole tribes and communities. The history of India up to the tenth Christian century is largely the history of the spread of Aryan religion and culture throughout the whole land. The conversion of a tribe to Hinduism meant its acknowledgment of the supremacy of the Brahmans and its enrolment as a separate caste in the Hindu system. These were the essentials. As regards religious faith and practice, the newly Hinduized tribe would be free to make any adjustment it pleased—usually a compromise between its own gods and the gods of the Hindu pantheon. Thus in the long process of the Aryanization of India, the non-Aryan peoples must have contributed to the joint stock of religious customs and traditions almost or quite as much as they received.

Now on similar terms Hinduism would be quite willing to absorb every people on earth. Hinduism presents itself as a kind of gigantic religious octopus which is ready to swallow up everything within its reach. Now there is syncretism and syncretism. No fault is to be found with the syncretism which proves all things and holds fast that which is good, whatever its source may be. Such syncretism is critical, and is one of the main sources of religious progress. But the syncretism of Hinduism is *uncritical.* The supreme tests for admission to the fold of Hinduism are not moral or intellectual, but *social*—the adoption of caste—organization and the acknowledgment of Brahman supremacy. The essential element in Hinduism, then, is not belief, but social organization. This fact explains why it is that the Hindu finds fault with the Christian missionary, not for preaching Christ in India, but only for *baptizing.* It is the disruption of the Hindu social system, rather than a change of belief, which is feared.

The Hindu tendency to syncretism explains also the interesting religious fusions which are the result in India of the meeting of different faiths. For example, *Sikhism* and the *Kabir-panth* are the fruit of the contact of Hinduism with Islam; and the Brahmo Samaj, Prarthna Samaj, Chet Rami Sect, and even the Arya Samaj and the Deva Samaj are the fruit of the similar contact of Hinduism with Christianity. Neo-Vedantism also represents the old Vedantism as modified by modern influences, especially by Christianity. Among the more notable Neo-Vedanta preachers who have visited the West both Swami Vivekananda and Swami Ram Tirath were graduates of Christian colleges.

C. A third characteristic of Hinduism is that it accepts and justifies a pronounced *contrast between priestly and popular religion.*

This contrast already appears in the earliest or

Vedic stratum of Hindu religion. The Rigveda (including the Sama and Yajur Vedas, which are largely extracts from the Rig) is on the whole hieratic or priestly. The Atharvaveda, on the other hand, is "demotic" and represents the magic practices, spells, and incantations, of popular religion. But notice that the Rigveda and the Atharvaveda were both received into the Hindu canon. The stamp of divine authority was affixed not only to the text-book of priestly religion but also to the text-book of popular religion. It is as if the Old Testament contained, in addition to the prophetic writings, an equal portion devoted to the popular practices of sorcery, incantation, and witchcraft as seen, for example, in the raising of Samuel by the witch of Endor. Prophetic religion in Old Testament times had a long, fierce struggle with popular religion, but there was never any such reconciliation with popular religion as is seen in the inclusion of both the Rigveda and the Atharvaveda in one (and that, too, the most sacred) canon of Hindu holy scripture. The Hindu sacred books which are accessible to the West through translations are, on the whole, repositories of hieratic religion,—the Four Vedas (including *Mantras, Brahmanas,* and Upanishads), the Law-books, the Six Systems of Philosophy, the Bhagavadgita, the Epics, etc. Popular religion consists of the more or less unwritten practice of the ignorant masses of India.[8] The most important doctrines of Hindu hieratic religion are the

[8] See Crooke's *Popular Religion of Northern India.*

doctrines of *Brahma* and *Maya,* the identity of the individual soul with the Supreme Soul, transmigration, and Karma. Usually the crudest form of popular religion has more or less of hieratic doctrine, especially the doctrines of transmigration and *Karma.* Here again the Hindu tendency to syncretism is illustrated. But the point to be emphasized is that the existence of popular religion, however crude and even immoral it may be, is justified by Hinduism on the ground that it represents a necessary stage of progress in the soul's development. And so there has been as yet no large effort on the part of learned Hinduism to correct the errors and crudities and immoralities of popular religion. It has been maintained that no interference is necessary since through the operation of transmigration and *Karma* every soul, however debased, will by means of repeated births finally attain to its proper goal. Hence extra-caste altruism has no real root in Hinduism as ordinarily held. The supreme duty of every man is faithfully to follow the rules of his caste.

D. A fourth characteristic of Hinduism is *the dominance of the religious point of view in all the affairs of life, or the supremacy of the religious consciousness.*

More fully perhaps in Hinduism than even in orthodox Judaism, religion embraces the whole of life. One explanation of this is that the separation which has been made in the West between social custom (with an Aryan origin) and religion (with a

Semitic origin) has never taken place in India. In the long course of the conversion of India to Hinduism each tribe and community brought into the Hindu system not only its religious practices but also its social customs and all alike received in time a religious sanction. The cake of custom has been broken in the West, but in the East it remains intact. Hence Christianity and Hinduism touch common life differently. The principle of Christianity is, "Whether ye eat or drink or whatsoever ye do, do all to the glory of God." (1 Cor. 10:31.) But the principle of Hinduism is, "Whether ye eat or drink or whatsoever ye do, do all" according to fixed rule and established custom. This explains in part why Eastern peoples in general and Hindus in particular seem at first sight so religious. It is because their religion consists so largely in the punctilious performance of an elaborate body of religiously consecrated custom touching every detail of life.

In view of this fact, the emphasis placed in recent days on the Hindu religious consciousness could properly bear some abatement. It remains true, nevertheless, that the Indian consciousness is primarily and fundamentally not political, economic, or artistic, but *religious*. The vast Sanskrit literature of India is predominantly religious. The great movements of India have been religious movements. India's influence on the outside world has been chiefly religious. The eminent characters of India, so far as recorded, have been religious. India has been religiously creative in the past and may again be so in the future. To this day, every strong religious personality in India cherishes the ambition of religious creativeness. All of which means that the people of India are richly endowed with the religious instinct and consciousness.

E. A fifth characteristic of Hinduism is *great reverence for the ideal of renunciation and great capacity for sacrifice.*

There is no other land on earth where there is such reverence for the religious mendicant and such readiness on the part of multitudes for a life of extreme hardship and even of self-inflicted torture as in India. But here too the reverence for the ideal of renunciation is often an undiscriminating one, responsible for the existence in India of no less than five millions of mendicants, vast numbers of whom are certainly not religious in any sense, and as a non-producing element in the population are a serious economic drag. In like manner the capacity for self-sacrifice in connection with religion has too often realized itself in selfish and unpractical ways, the religious devotee usually being supremely concerned about his personal salvation alone, and seeking it by a process of self-annihilation rather than of self-development. But when India's religious creativeness, spiritual passion, and capacity for sacrifice become linked to worthy ends, then the long travail of India's religious experience will finally justify itself by bearing much fruit. In any event, the ideal of renunciation for spiritual ends and the capacity for sacrifice must be reckoned among the spiritual assets of Hinduism.

F. A sixth characteristic of Hinduism is *the existence in it of aspirations and anticipations still largely unfulfilled and unsatisfied.*

Such aspirations appear already in the Rigveda. Practically every one of the nine or ten hymns addressed to Varuna contains a confession of sin and a cry for pardon. Of the ten incarnations of Vishnu, nine according to Hindu belief have already come and the tenth as contrasted with all the rest is to be a *Nishkalankh Avatara,* or sinless incarnation. It is a testimony to the Hindu hope that the final incarnation as sinless will deal adequately with the problem of sin.

The profoundest formula of the most rigidly monistic type of the Vedanta is *Aham Brahma,* "I am Brahma."[4] Whatever else this formula may mean, it voices the aspiration of many of the saintliest thinkers of India for a union with Deity so close as to be equivalent to *identity.* It expresses the longing of the Indian heart for release from the trammels of the phenomenal world, and participation in the changeless perfection of the Absolute.

[4] The formula *Aham Brahma* may be interpreted as the fulfilment of aspiration on the part of those who are able to use it as a fundamental article of faith or, in other words, as a formula of spiritual realisation. For the vast majority of Hindus, however, it remains "a counsel of perfection" too hard of attainment here and now by the average man, but nevertheless longed for and expected ultimately in the course of repeated births.

Such then is Hinduism in barest outline. As we have seen, Hinduism is a generic term for the totality of the religious and social customs found in India, so far as they are organized by the adoption of caste and the recognition of the social and religious supremacy of the Brahmans. As a system, Hinduism is as vast and amorphous as the sea. It is based upon a radical theory of the immanence of God in all things. Its method of growth and development is through syncretism. Its whole tendency has been to touch with religious sanction whatever is, consecrating some of the worst things as well as the best. But at the same time the vast and chaotic fabric of Hinduism is shot through with profound ideas and illuminated here and there with lofty aspirations and splendid gleams of insight. Hinduism has always been rich in scholars and ascetic saints.

CHAPTER III

THE THEISTIC HINDUISM OF RAMANUJA

RAMANUJA lived far south in India. Like many of the greatest Indian philosophers and theologians, he belonged to the Dravidian area and probably carried Dravidian blood in his veins. Though he lived in the eleventh century A.D., the important school that he founded exists today, and so is worthy of being considered among the aspects of contemporary Hinduism.

Indian philosophy began with the problem of the universe as a whole. The aim was to discover the principle of unity in plurality. In the Vedic stage it was declared to be *Purusha;* in the Brahmanic, *Prajapati;* and in the Upanishadic, *Brahman,* each in turn being pronounced "all this," that is equated with the whole universe.[1] Thus there was multiplicity for experience, but in some sense or other unity for thought.

In the Upanishads there was manifested a tendency to divide the universe viewed as the undifferentiated *brahman* into two categories: brahman formed and brahman formless, mortal and immortal, phenom-

[1] *Rv.* X, 90, 2; *Shat. Br.* V, 1, 1, 4; *Chhand. Up.* III, 14, 1.

enal and noumenal, defined and undefined, conditioned and unconditioned, timed and timeless.[2] These contrasted categories raised the further question of how the phenomenal is related to the noumenal, the many to the one. There are three moments in the solution. Plurality is, represents the Vedic thesis; unity is, the Upanishadic antithesis; and the final synthesis exists in two forms, plurality is the illusive play of Unity (Shankara), or plurality is a manifestation of Unity and participates in its reality (Ramanuja).

This introduces us to the rival schools of the rigid non-dualism of Shankara (eighth century) and the qualified non-dualism of Ramanuja (eleventh century). Shankara and Ramanuja had much in common. They both held a high doctrine of the authority of the Upanishads. They both were commentators and philosophical theologians; they were both masters of the art of rational disputation. Their differences were differences in interpretation of the meaning of scripture.

Take the great monistic text, "One only without a second." [3] Both theologians agree that there is only one being in the universe who possesses primary reality, or, as the late Professor Oldenberg puts it, "the

[2] See Hume's *Thirteen Principal Upanishads*, pp. 97, 287, and Griswold's *Brahman*, p. 71. We are reminded of Spinoza's *Natura naturata* and *Natura naturans*, Kant's phenomenon and noumenon, and Schopenhauer's Idea and Will. See also Radhakrishnan's *Indian Philosophy*, Vol. I.

[3] *Chhand. Up.* VI, 2, 1.

highest degree of reality."[4] But they differ absolutely in their conception of secondary reality. Shankara denied that anything except the fullest reality is real, all else being cast into the limbo of the unreal. For to him absolute, unconditioned and necessary being is the hall-mark of reality. Ramanuja, on the other hand, accepted various levels of the real on the principle that reality is "a thing of degrees."[5] Thus for Ramanuja the contrast was between independent and dependent reality; for Shankara, between complete reality and illusion, Brahman and *maya.* Shankara's unity is the unity of a bare naked monad, while Ramanuja's is the unity of a system. The one is an idealistic theory pushed to the utmost extreme; the other is comparatively realistic.

Ramanuja, like Dayanand Sarasvati, Agnihotri, and the father of Pandita Ramabai, was early trained in the strict Vedanta of Shankara, and like them soon threw overboard absolute non-dualism in favor of the more common-sense view of qualified non-dualism.[6] For Ramanuja the debate was no mere philosophical controversy, but in very truth, as Professor Otto phrases it, "a struggle for God,"[7] that is to say, for a personal God in place of the impersonal *brahma.* Shankara, too, admitted a personal god grasped by

[4] *Lehre der Upanishaden,* 1915, p. 84.

[5] *Brahman,* p. 50.

[6] Ramanuja's revolt in Hinduism against the force of Shankara's logic reminds of Wesley's similar revolt in Christianity against Calvin's equally abstract and relentless logic. For Shankara there was a single Being in the universe; for Calvin, a single Will.

[7] *India's Religion of Grace,* p. 29.

the "lower knowledge," but a god just as unreal in the ultimate analysis as anything else within the sphere of *maya*. For Shankara held that the impersonal is a higher category than the personal and hence the idea of a personal god must finally yield to the true conception of Ultimate Reality as impersonal. Said a follower of Shankara to Dr. Otto: "You Christians are the same as our *bhaktas*. Your relation to God is that of a child to his father.[8] We also approve that. Still, the true and final completion of the *ekata-bhava,* the relation of complete unity and oneness with God, lies far above and beyond it."[9] Hence fundamentally Ramanuja's struggle against Shankara's conception of *brahma* was a struggle to establish the real and eternal personality of God.

The distinction in the field of epistemology between the "higher" and the "lower" knowledge was championed by Shankara. Mind working, as Shankara held, under the power of *avidya,* "nescience," produces the consciousness of multiplicity and with it the various gods of religion. This *avidya* is a kind of "total depravity" of the intellect.[10] For the intellect persists in superimposing upon the one reality the *upadhis,* "limiting adjuncts," or, in Kantian

[8] Compare Rabindranath Tagore's *Morning Prayer* as quoted by Thompson, *Rabindranath Tagore,* p. 97.

[9] *India's Religion of Grace,* pp. 21-22. Ramanuja taught a "personal Vedanta." See Prof. Otto's *"Die Methoden des Erweises der Seele im personalem Vedanta"* in *Zeitschrift für Religionspsychologie.*

[10] Corresponding to the "total depravity" of the will, as held by a certain school of Christian thinkers.

phrase, time, space and causality, with the result that the fundamentally unreal appearance of multiplicity is created.[11] *Maya* is the network of illusion spun like a spider's web out of the very texture of the mind itself. For the "higher knowledge," however, all multiplicity, including the gods, even the highest god of human thought, disappears. It is the removing of the things that are shaken, that "those things which cannot be shaken may remain" (Hebrews XII, 27). And the sole survivor of the crash of worlds is Brahman, "the one only without a second." Such is Shankara's view.

Ramanuja rejected Shankara's theory of knowledge, holding that the testimony of the senses is broadly trustworthy and therefore proves that the multiplicity of things, including ourselves, is real. Shankara's "lower knowledge" is knowledge through the senses and through reasoning on the data of sense, a knowledge which he pronounces illusory. His "higher knowledge" seems to mean faith in the great utterances of the Upanishads as interpreted by himself, defended by reason, and realized in experience. So we have in Shankara's "higher knowledge" at once a doctrine of scripture and a doctrine of faith. Just as the Christian is to "reckon himself (*ethically*) dead unto sin, but alive unto God" on the basis of the scripture to that effect (Rom. VI, 11), even so the follower of Shankara is to reckon himself *metaphysically* separate from all plurality and identical

[11] *Brahman*, p. 73.

with Brahma on the basis of such scripture texts as *Tat twam asi,* "That art thou."

Ramanuja does not deny the text, "That art thou;" he interprets it in another way. Shankara presses conclusions to the uttermost. *"Thou,"* which covers the multiplicity of souls, since it is applicable to any and every soul, must reduce to the one Soul in order to be equated with "that," namely the ultimate reality *brahman,* which is clearly "one only without a second." But, says Ramanuja in his argument against this view, God is myself just as my soul is the self of my body. As the soul supports the body, so God is the supporter and "inner guide" of my soul. He is the Soul of my soul and the Soul of all souls. The world, including all souls, constitutes the body of the Lord in the sense that it is indwelt by Him and is absolutely dependent upon Him. Thus God and the world form a system, God being immanent in the world and the world sharing to some degree in the reality of God. The relations between the Infinite Spirit and the finite spirit are personal. It is the mysterious communion of life with life, but never identity of the created with the Creator.[12] Such is what might be called Ramanuja's "higher knowledge," his doctrine of faith in the Upanishad scripture as interpreted by himself, defended by reason, and realized in experience. In this sense the doctrine of a twofold knowledge is common to all religions, faith being taken as a "higher knowledge." [13]

[12] *India's Religion of Grace,* pp. 39-40.

[13] Prof. Otto calls this "higher knowledge," "faith-knowledge." See *The Idea of the Holy,* Eng. trans., 1925, pp. 226-227.

Ramanuja held to the doctrines of transmigration and karma, but he made the grace of God superior to both. The personality of both God and man is maintained and the end of the process of salvation is viewed, not as a losing of one's identity in God, but as eternal fellowship with Him. God as personal is endowed with all noble attributes and this guarantees the centrality of the ethical. There is no state "beyond good and evil." Thus Ramanuja laid strong foundations in Hinduism for a theistic conception of God. In fact, "he presents to us the highest intellectual altitude reached in all its varied history by Indian Theism."[14]

The absolute *advaita* of Shankara is commonly regarded as the religion of India *par excellence*. This is far from being true, although with the Hindu flair for syncretism ideas belonging to the strict *advaita* of Shankara are often combined with other systems of thought which are opposed to rigid non-dualism.

Ramanuja in his soteriology magnified two things, objectively the *grace*—unmerited favor—of God, and subjectively *faith*, the attitude of *bhakti*, trustful and obedient love. There is emphasis on *ekagrata*, "one-pointedness," "singleness of aim." It is the seeking of God with one's whole heart. And this singleness of attitude is made effective, not by the strength of man, but by the grace of God. Thus the system of Ramanuja well deserves the name of evangelical Hinduism.

[14] Dr. Macnicol's *Indian Theism*, p. 107.

CHAPTER IV

KESHAB CHANDER SEN AND THE CHURCH OF THE "NEW DISPENSATION"

THE Brahmo [1] Samaj, or "Society of God," represents the first religious reaction of India to the impact of the West. It was founded in Calcutta, 1824, by the Brahman, Ram Mohan Roy (d. 1833), a contemporary of the early missionaries, Carey, Marshman, Ward, and Duff. He was a child of the nineteenth-century Indian renascence, knowing Bengali, Sanskrit, Persian, Arabic, English, and some Greek and Hebrew. The renascence in his case was followed by reformation, at once religious in the form of the Brahmo Samaj, and social in the strenuous efforts he made against polygamy and "sati" and in favor of the marriage of Hindu widows. Through his knowledge of the literature and religion of both India and Britain, Ram Mohan Roy was fitted to be a mediator between the East and the West. He had a keen appreciation of Christian ethics, as witness his book, *The Precepts of Jesus, the Guide to Peace and Happiness,* but he undervalued the exercise of *prayer.* Like Swami Dayanand, he was rationalistic and non-mystical, and

[1] Spelled Brahma but pronounced Brahmo. Hence the form *Brahmo* is used.

his system was deistic in type rather than theistic. In fact, the religious experience of Ram Mohan Roy is a kind of replica of that of Swami Dayanand. Both revolted from idolatry at an early age, both clung to the Vedic hymns, and both sought to restore Hindu worship to its pristine purity.

Under the leadership of Debendra Nath Tagore significant changes were made. The Samaj became more theistic. Prayer was introduced, but, strange to say, Debendra Nath, like his son Rabindra Nath, had little use for Christ, even as a moral teacher. The tendency of the society to become a Vedic sect was halted by the work of a committee of scholars which reported on the Four Vedas with the result that the infallibility of the Vedic literature was rejected. Thus the Brahmo Samaj was thrown back on natural religion.

In 1850 the faith of the Samaj was summed up in six propositions. God (1) is a personal being, (2) has never become incarnate, (3) hears and answers prayer, (4) is to be worshipped only in spiritual ways, (5) forgives and saves those who repent and cease from sin and (6) is known through nature and intuition. There is no mention yet of the *Fatherhood* of God or the *immortality* of the human spirit.

Keshab Chander Sen joined the Brahmo Samaj in 1857. Ram Mohan Roy and Debendra Nath were Brahmans; Keshab was by caste a *Vaidya* (physician), and by sect a *Vaishnava*. He had a good modern education. He had suffered from religious melancholy but had found peace through prayer. He soon threw himself strenuously into the work of the Samaj, and enjoyed five years of happy fellowship with Debendra Nath (1859-1865). The year 1861 was marked by the self-dedication to full time service of Keshab and others, which meant self-sacrifice. We are reminded of the "great vow" of Pandit Agnihotri.

The immemorial prejudice in favor of Brahman leadership in religion now began to manifest itself. Keshab, a non-Brahman, was ordained an *Acharya* (minister), and some of the older members withdrew. It was the beginning of a cleft between Keshab the liberal, and Debendra, the conservative. Keshab thought that Debendra was holding back too much, since he disliked intercaste marriages and the marriage of widows, and in general regarded social questions as secondary. Debendra thought Keshab was going too fast. The immediate cause of the breach, however, was the re-assumption of the sacred thread by those leading in worship in spite of the agreement that no minister should be allowed to wear it. An ultimatum was sent by Keshab and his party, in February, 1865, that caused the final division. It was a youth movement, Keshab being twenty-four and Debendra forty-seven.

Keshab's society was launched with the reading of theistic texts from Hindu, Buddhist, Christian, Muhammadan, Zoroastrian, and Confucian scriptures. It was a kind of "universal theism" based on the religious scriptures of the world. Keshab had recently read Dean Stanley's *Works,* Robertson's *Sermons,* Liddon's *Divinity of Our Lord, Theologia Germanica,* and Seeley's *Ecce Homo.* A fruit of these readings in Christian literature was a lecture that he delivered in 1866 on *"Jesus Christ: Europe and Asia,"* drawing attention to the fact that Jesus was an Asiatic and stressing his moral precepts after the manner of Ram Mohan Roy.[2] Keshab's enthusiasm for the character of Jesus led many to believe that he was about to become a Christian. Not long before this a preaching tour in South India had helped to enlarge the thoughts of Keshab. His visit to Madras resulted in the founding of the *Veda-Samaj* (1864); and at Bombay as a consequence of his visit, the *Parthana Samaj,* or "Society of Prayer," was organized (1867).

The breach resulted in the *Adi Brahmo Samaj,* or "Original Society," Debendra Nath's organization, more Hindu than before, and Keshab's new society, the *Brahmo Samaj of India.* Keshab stressed the need of propaganda. He had seven or eight disciples who followed him in enthusiasm and self-sacrifice. For purposes of worship he introduced certain Vaishnava innovations, in which *bhakti* (loving devotion) was emphasized, including *nagarkirtan* (town-praise), a kind of singing procession, and *sankirtan* (chorus singing, with instruments). He also introduced annual festivals and a "spiritual retreat."

In 1867, Keshab delivered in Calcutta a lecture on

[2] Later Pratap Chander Mozoomdar followed the same line of thought and published *The Oriental Christ.*

"Great Men," the purpose of which was to correct the misapprehensions created by his lecture on "Jesus Christ," and also to give expression to his latest views on revelation. Debendra Nath had recognized two sources of the Knowledge of God—Nature and Intuition. Keshab added a third source, God in history, speaking through great men. Many naturally began to infer that Keshab was laying a foundation for the claim that he himself was an organ of revelation.

Keshab was to see still more of the world. He visited Simla, the summer capital of India, and had an interview with Lord Lawrence, the Governor-General. In 1870, like Ram Mohan Roy, he suddenly determined to go to England. There he had an audience with Queen Victoria; he carried back from England a deep impression of the value of the Christian home.

Besides the efforts toward the education of girls, emancipation of women, remarriage of widows, marriage between persons of different castes and the struggle against child marriage, there was brought about as a great social and legislative triumph The Brahmo Marriage Act of 1872, which was a distinct instrument of reform within the Brahmo Samaj. Positively, it abolished early marriage, made polygamy an offense, and sanctioned widow remarriage and intercaste marriage, but, negatively, it alienated from the Brahmo Samajists the sympathies of their orthodox countrymen.

During this period of his greatest influence (1872-

1878), Keshab met Swami Dayanand, who was soon to found the Arya Samaj. He made the acquaintance also of that strange religious devotee, Ramakrishna—this was the meeting of a Hindu modernist with a Hindu fundamentalist. Each, nevertheless, had a warm admiration for the other. New forms of devotion represent the possible influence of the illiterate saint of Dakshineshwar over Keshab, such as *Vairagya* (separation from the world), asceticism, and fresh vows of poverty.

Keshab in his turn introduced Ramakrishna to the world, and opened up to him such a sphere of influence over the educated young men of Calcutta as resulted in the establishment of the Vedanta Society in the West.

As Keshab had opposed Debendra Nath, so there arose a group in his own Samaj to oppose him. In one matter he was conservative. He was afraid of the effect of freedom and higher education on women, while many of his followers were determined to give their daughters a modern education. Then, too, Keshab was an autocrat. He ruled the whole Samaj as the sole authority. He objected to every form of popular government proposed. His doctrine of *adesh* (command) meant that a direct command from God had been laid on him by special revelation. He apparently favored those who regarded him as the divinely commissioned leader of the movement. Some of his youthful followers began to fall at his feet. Serious protests were raised, and two of the Brahmo missionaries actually left Keshab.

The Kuch-Bihar marriage brought the friction to a head. The young prince of Kuch-Bihar and Keshab's daughter were both under age in the sight of the Brahmo marriage law.[3] Since the Kuch-Bihar family were Hindus, the prince could not be married as a Brahmo member. It would have to be a Hindu marriage under which the prince might take other wives. Now Keshab had been fighting child-marriage for years, it was through his influence that the Brahmo Marriage Act was passed, and by this arrangement Keshab would be made to violate his own law.

Keshab found it very difficult to refuse his consent. Though the Government was eager to see the marriage brought about, the young prince declared that he was a theist, that he would not take other wives. The Government extracted promises that everything idolatrous would be excluded. So Keshab consented, with the understanding that the wedding would be in reality only a betrothal and that the ceremony would contain nothing idolatrous. His consent, too, was buttressed by his doctrine of *adesh,* the command of God. The result was that a large body of the best members left the Samaj.

[3] According to the Brahmo Marriage Act of 1872 the minimum age for marriage is eighteen years for men and fourteen for women (the same as that of the Sarda Act of 1930); but young people according to the Brahmo Act, must get the written consent of their parents, if they marry before the age of twenty-one.

At the time of the second schism (1878) there were one hundred and twenty-four local congregations in existence, most of them connected with Keshab's Samaj. The *Adi* (Original) *Samaj* still continued, but the ground lost at the first schism never had been recovered. Debendra Nath Tagore retired in 1872, his son Dvijendra, brother of Rabindra Nath Tagore, succeeding him. In the second schism the majority of the provincial Samajes sided with the protesting party, and so Keshab lost the major part of his membership.

The name assumed by the protesting party in 1878 was the *Sadharan Brahmo Samaj,* the word *sadharan* meaning "general." It was organized on the basis of representative government. It is interesting to observe, however, that Pandit S. N. Agnihotri of Lahore, one of the first ordained ministers of the Sadharan Samaj, ultimately followed Keshab in the matter of autocracy. The most prominent leader of the protesting Samaj was Pandit Shiva Nath Shastri. Three articles of faith were added to the six of the Original Samaj: (1) the fatherhood of God and the brotherhood of man, (2) the immortality and eternal progress of the soul, and (3) the remedial and not eternal nature of God's punishments of sin.

Keshab also adopted a new name for his Samaj, *Nava Vidhana,* the "New Dispensation," which was proclaimed in January, 1881. The suggestions of Christian influence are numerous, the very name "New Dispensation" reminding one of the Christian contrast between the "Old" Dispensation and the "New." On the great day of the proclamation Keshab had twelve missionaries around him—his Twelve Apostles—and a new banner was set up containing trident, cross, and crescent. On the table lay the four great scriptures of the world, Hindu, Buddhist, Christian, Muhammadan. Four were appointed, each to study the scriptures of one of the religions. Henceforth Keshab's Society was called "The Church of the New Dispensation." It was declared to be God's latest revelation, a new gospel to complete and harmonize all existing religions. And of this New Dispensation Keshab Chander Sen was the prophet and medium of revelation, possessing, as he claimed, a special divine commission. He said in his address, "It has pleased the holy God to send into the world a message of peace and love, of harmony and reconciliation." Later, in 1884, Keshab announced: "Let Asia, Europe, Africa, and America, with diverse instruments, praise the New Dispensation and sing the Fatherhood of God and the Brotherhood of man."

Keshab's final system incorporated some striking Hindu innovations. His friend, Ramakrishna, held that "all religions are true." In harmony with this is Keshab's statement: "Our position is not that truths are to be found in all religions, but that *all the established religions of the world are true.*"[4] It was a great change from Keshab's early days, when he

[4] As printed in *The Sunday Mirror,* Oct. 23, 1881. See Farquhar, *Modern Religious Movements in India,* p. 57.

believed that all coquetting with other systems was dangerous. "Dishonest latitudinarianism" was the term applied to it in 1873 by the General Religious Association. Besides, Keshab adopted certain Hindu ceremonies and Hindu doctrines. He called God "Mother"—the same way that Ramakrishna used to call Kali "Mother." He adopted the *homa,* or Vedic sacrifice, and the *arati,* or fire-waving ceremony. He introduced Chaitanya's religious dance. Further, he found spiritual nourishment in the *Durga Puja* (the worship of Durga), and expounded polytheism and idolatry as if they were variant forms of theism.

Innovations drawn from Christianity, notably the ceremonies of Baptism and the Lord's Supper, were introduced into the ritual of the New Dispensation Church. In his early lectures Keshab went far beyond Ram Mohan Roy in his estimate of Jesus, and in three directions: there was the fullest recognition of the glory of the *character* of Christ; of the sinless Christ as the creator of the sense of sin; and of the Christ who "went about doing good" as the source of the Christian attitude toward social life. "We may justly ascribe this passion for social reform," writes a historian of the Brahmo Samaj, "to the influence of Mr. Sen's Christian studies. The reason for my ascribing it to Christian influence is that it is so unlike the Hindu teaching on the subject, with which we are familiar." These three aspects of Christ, namely, his righteous character, the effect of his character in producing the sense of sin, and its effect also in creating an enthusiasm for social righteousness, constituted the very pith and marrow of Keshab's doctrine.

Before leaving India in 1926, I presided at a meeting of the Lahore Brahmo Samaj on the occasion of the anniversary of the birth of Keshab Chander Sen. One of the speakers, Professor Ruchi Ram, M.A., alluding to the Christian aspects of Keshab's doctrine and practice, denied that he was in any real sense a Christian. One has only to recall the henotheistic atmosphere of the Vedic hymns in order to find the explanation. Each Vedic tribe had its god or gods. These, in consequence of an Aryan federation, political or religious, were brought together in worship as a kind of consolidated pantheon. A *rishi,* or hymn-writer, could select from the whole pantheon of gods that one god whom he was in a mood to celebrate, and sing the praises of his *ishta devata,* as if he were the only god. But for Keshab's society the pantheon of Vedic gods had been so enlarged as to become the federation of all the gods and all the religions of the world. And the same henotheistic attitude as characterized the poets of the Rigveda doubtless held in the case of Keshab's admiration for Christ. It represented a *mood* rather than the settled conviction of his life. If in any respect Christ was superior to other great religious teachers in the thought of Keshab, it was as a *primus inter pares,* not as the one unique revelation of God.

The creed of Keshab's Church had come to embrace twelve articles, six from the undivided Samaj of 1850, three from the Sadharan Samaj (1878), and three which were peculiar to the New Dispensation. These last three were: (1) God is a Trinity in Unity —Father, Son, and Spirit—God being Mother as well as Father; (2) Brahmoism is not a new religion, but the essence of all religions, the one universal faith, because the Brahmo Samaj is God's latest Dispensation and its missionaries are the God-appointed apostles of the new gospel; and (3) the knowledge of God comes through inspired men as well as through nature and intuition. God reveals His will on occasion to His servants by command, *adesh*. In all this the explicit claim is only that Keshab's Samaj is "God's latest Dispensation," but the claim is implicit and unmistakable that Keshab himself is the mediator of the New Dispensation, God's mouthpiece for introducing "the one universal faith."

In 1884 the total number of congregations belonging to the three branches of the Brahmo Samaj were 173; covenanted members about 1,500, and adherents about 8,000. In 1901 there were 4,050 members according to the Indian Census, and in 1921, 6,388. It may be remarked that the influence of the Brahmo Samaj vastly transcends its statistical significance.

CHAPTER V

RAMAKRISHNA, THE ILLITERATE SAINT OF BENGAL

IN RAMAKRISHNA PARAMAHANSA there is presented the marvel of an illiterate teacher of college-bred disciples. Ramakrishna (1836-1886) was a contemporary of Swami Dayanand (1824-1883), and Keshab Chander Sen (1839-1884), but, unlike these two radical reformers, he clung to the end to the old Hindu ways, including Tantrism and Kali-worship. He thus represents Hindu fundamentalism.

Gadadhar Chatterji was a Bengali Brahman, born in the village of Kamarpukar, by sect a Vishnuite, his name, Gadadhar (club-bearer), being one of the names of Vishnu. As a lad he ran wild and played truant from school. He learned no Sanskrit, little English, and very imperfect Bengali. His means of early culture were religious stories, the acting of religious dramas, and the companionship of wandering Hindu ascetics. His life story teems with marvels. He was, we are told, miraculously conceived. His Vaishnava heritage of emotionalism and mysticism began early to manifest itself in strange psychic phenomena, such as ecstasy and trance.

Soon, his father having died, he had to earn his own living. But what was he to do, he who had no training? There was one post open to him, the priesthood.[1] So he became an assistant in a temple at Dakshineshvara near Calcutta, his task being to decorate with flowers the image of the goddess Kali.[2] In the worship of this fierce goddess with her garland of skulls, girdle of human arms, and naked sword, Gadadhar displayed a marvellous capacity for idealization. She was for him "the mother of the universe" and "his own mother." He would talk and sing to her by the hour. In every crisis of his life he would turn to her for guidance. "To this sombre divinity, whom Romain Rolland describes as 'a purring tigress,' Ramakrishna dedicated his life." [3]

[1] The business of a *pujari* (temple-priest), like that of a cook, seems to be the economic refuge of illiterate Brahmans. For as Baines tells us (*Ethnology*, 1912, p. 27): "Service in a temple . . . is not undertaken by the better class of Brahmans, as it is held to be degrading, and left accordingly, to those low-in station. . . . The inference drawn from this estimation of temple service is that the divinities in question are those of the non Arya." Quite in the same way Keith (Art. *Priesthood*, E. R. E.) remarks: "At the lowest level stands the village priest." I have interviewed many *pujaris*, especially in Kashmir, but have never found one who knew Sanskrit. Most of them are entirely illiterate.

[2] *Kali*, "the Black" was originally a Dravidian goddess as contrasted with the fair Aryan gods. She is a *Devi Mata*, "mother goddess," unlike the predominantly masculine Aryan deities. The ethnological composition of Bengal is declared by Risley to be Aryo-Dravidian with an infusion of Mongolian blood. The ethnological complex was followed by religious synthesis, the Dravidian Kali being adopted into the Aryan pantheon. Kali is a nature goddess, setting forth at once the fierce and terrible side of nature and its kindly aspect, but with a large emphasis on the former. See the description of Kali in M. K. Gandhi's *Autobiography* and also in Miss Mayo's *Mother India*. "There is much about Kali that suggests the raptures of the devotees of Voodoo" (Charles Johnston in *N. Y. Times*, Nov. 9, 1930).

[3] Charles Johnston in his review of *Prophets of the New India*, *N. Y. Times*, Nov. 9, 1930.

Along with this passionate worship of the *image*[4] of Kali went also experiences of trance, or "falling sickness,"[5] times of coma and bodily rigidity.

Soon his mother and his brothers began to say, "He is beside himself," and they fixed upon the usual cure for such cases of other-worldliness, namely *marriage*. It was a marriage of conservative Hinduism, the bridegroom twenty-five and the bride five. But they did not live together: the priestly bridegroom went back at once to the temple and the little girl returned to her father's house. In fact they never lived together as husband and wife. Later she became his devoted pupil, and he thought of her only as his mother, an embodiment of Mother Kali. It looks like a case of mother-fixation.

Gadadhar had tended the visible image of Kali, dressing and decorating it, and had experienced times of ecstasy regarded by him as evidences of "possession" by Mother Kali, but he desired to see

[4] There are two possible views of idol worship in Hinduism. The first is the merely symbolical use of the image to fix the attention and awaken devout thought. This view I once heard explained and defended by a Swami at the Vedanta Center in New York City. Another view is involved in the ceremony of consecrating an image (*prana-pratishtha*, "life-implanting"). It yields an entirely different conception, reminding one of the Roman Catholic doctrine of transubstantiation. See *Images and Idols* (Indian) by Crooke, E.R.E., 1915, and *Rites of the Twice-born* by Margaret Stevenson, 1920, pp. 409-415. Probably Gadadhar, the acolyte in the temple of Kali, held the second view as well as the first, for Max Müller in his book, *Ramakrishna* (1898), which is based on the material furnished by Vivekananda, writes: "He [Gadadhar] believed it [the image] to be living and breathing and taking food out of his hand" (p. 57).

[5] Charles Johnston in the review mentioned above remarks: "Romain Rolland does not seem to realize how sinister and dangerous is the whole of Ramakrishna's experience."

"greater things than these," even a vision of the invisible Kali. So he gave himself to prayer and tears and unearthly yearning, until the vision came. But such excess of ecstasy as he experienced left him unconscious for hours; he neglected his work, and so lost his position. He settled down in a neighboring wood, where for twelve years he gave himself to strenuous prayer and effort toward self-conquest, his supreme aim being to attain union with God. In his intense and prolonged effort to realize union with the Divine, Ramakrishna was an embodiment of the spirit of India. He sought this high end with the same absolute devotion that a Western captain of industry gives to the building up of his business.

Now appeared upon the scene the *Bhairavi Brahmani*, a devotee of the fearful Kali. This Brahmani nun understood Gadadhar and he found in her a new object for mother worship. She had Vaishnava books which told the story of Chaitanya, and as she explained it, the madness of both Chaitanya and Gadadhar was a "madness[6] after God." Thus she comforted him, and not only so, but proceeded as a kind of Hindu Priscilla to "expound unto him the way of God more perfectly." She taught him the Tantric methods of realization, and especially the Tantric Yoga[7] with its strange doctrines of the

[6] Wendell Thomas's *Hinduism Invades America*, 1930, p. 51.

[7] About the time when Dayanand Sarasvati was testing the Tantric Yoga by the dissection of a corpse and throwing, as a result, the dissected corpse and the discredited Tantric books into the river, Ramakrishna was meekly swallowing the whole as mother's milk from the breast of his Brahmani preceptress.

Kundalini, the *Sushumna* and the six lotuses. Then having taught her spiritual son all she knew, the Bhairavi nun went her way.

Next came the naked ascetic Totapuri, who also made his contribution to the spiritual development of Gadadhar. He taught him the monistic doctrine of Shankara—that God is impersonal, the soul identical with God, and the world an illusion. He taught him the highest stage of religious trance, in which no sense of consciousness remains, "name and form," the products of Maya, being blotted out by the deep sleep which is the very image of reality. Gadadhar was initiated by him as a *sannyasi* with a new name,[8] Ramakrishna, to which his friends later added the title "Paramahansa." The net result of Totapuri's instruction was the distinction which Gadadhar grasped between the Supreme Being as inactive, impersonal and unqualified by attributes, and the same Supreme Being as active, personal, and qualified by attributes—the distinction, to wit, between Brahma and the Divine Mother. The impersonal and the personal may be distinguished but they, Ramakrishna held, are both true, because one and the same. In this way he sought to harmonize the divergent positions of Shankara and Ramanuja. The result of these new thoughts and experiences, we are told, was a prolonged trance which was followed by an equally

[8] Mul Shankar was also initiated into a Sannyasi order with the new name Dayananda Sarasvati. He retained the name to the end but unlike Gadadhar gave up the Vedantic doctrine of God.

prolonged attack of dysentery. Totapuri, having delivered his message, left like the Bhairavi Brahmani, never to return.

By family tradition Ramakrishna was a Vishnuite, and the Bhairavi Brahmani had explained his ecstatic experiences as similar to those of Chaitanya the great Vishnuite sage. He had already had a vision of the ethical Rama, chief incarnation of Vishnu, but he now yearned to realize more fully the Vishnuite ideal of passionate love for God, as set forth in the story of Lord Krishna. His method of realization was that of dramatic imitation, wearing woman's clothes and imagining himself to be Radha. It worked. He saw in vision the beautiful form of Krishna, and was satisfied.

Ramakrishna was now thirty-five years old. He had already experienced the various ways of reaching God, by the worship of the personal Kali, Rama and Krishna and by self-identification with, and meditation on, the impersonal and qualityless Brahma.[9] He was convinced that these different ways were all true. He was now prepared to extend his religious researches beyond Hinduism. First, he sought by the familiar method of dramatic imitation to understand Islam. To this end he became temporarily a Muhammadan in dress, manner of life, and religious practice. It worked. He soon had a

[9] Brahma, sometimes written "Brahm," is frequently used rather than the correct form Brahman, or brahman, to denote the impersonal world-ground, because it is more clearly understood by the Western reader.

vision in the trance state of a man with a long beard and serious countenance, presumably Muhammad. In like manner he tested Christianity. He read the Bible with a friend and saw a picture of the Madonna and Child. It was not long before he saw Jesus in a vision and was filled with the thought of His love. The conclusion was irresistible: all religions, Hinduism, Islam, Christianity and the rest, are true, because all alike, when tested, yielded to him the same ecstatic bliss in connection with the vision of their Founders.

Ramakrishna's greatest intellectual achievement was the solution (to his mind at least) of certain stubborn antinomies, such as the contrast between the personal and the impersonal conception of Ultimate Reality; between the Supreme Being, as active or inactive, dynamic or static; the antithesis between the ethical and the unethical; and the contrast between Hinduism and all the other religions of the world. Ramakrishna concluded that "the impersonal and the personal are one," that the unqualified and the qualified are one. As he phrases it, "At one time I am clothed, at another naked, so Brahman is at one time with attributes, and at another without." Brahman the static and Maya the dynamic are one, a unity which provides a basis for the activity of the good citizen, and especially for the inactivity and brooding calm of the sage. "Maya may be compared to a snake that is alive and moving, while Brahman is like the snake absolutely still." Both the ethical and the unethical are rooted in a unity which is "beyond good and evil." All religions are different paths to the same God, therefore "every man should follow his own religion." For the many religions all share in the truth and sacredness of the One Religion, of which they are varying expressions.

So much for the intellectual side of Ramakrishna's gospel. How far had he wrought out in experience its *moral* side? During the twelve years of stress and strain when he received tuition from the Brahmani nun and the naked ascetic Totapuri, he had struggled to free himself from the greed of gold, and the lust of woman. He seems to have succeeded. He came to loathe the very touch of money, and when his wife came to him as his disciple he maintained with her a platonic relation untouched by passion. A woman of the streets would only remind him of the "Divine Mother" in a different guise. One moral victory still remained to be won. What about the stubborn social cleft between caste and outcaste? Could he solve this antinomy? As a *sannyasi* he had no caste left, but as a Brahman by descent he had plenty of caste feeling. In order to destroy such prejudices, he played the part of a scavenger and cleansed the temple latrines; [10] he also ate the leavings of beggars and outcastes. This involved, however, no social disapprobation, since those who in the estimation of the Hindu people are the holiest,

[10] Compare the similar experience of Mahatma Gandhi as set forth in his *Autobiography*, Vol. I.

namely the *sannyasi* saints, are casteless. Still Ramakrishna's step to free himself once for all from caste prejudices and so to realize the oneness of humanity had real ethical value.

Having attained maturity in age (thirty-six), in mystical experience, in intellectual conviction, and in moral achievement, Ramakrishna was now prepared for larger contacts. One of the first to meet him at this time was Swami Dayanand Sarasvati. But though both were Brahmans, they were utterly unlike in temperament, and so their interview was devoid of any mutual influence. Three years later there occurred a meeting, pregnant with big issues, between Ramakrishna and Keshab Chander Sen. Though they differed in caste, they had the same Vishnuite heritage and mystical temperament. It was Keshab Chander Sen more than any one else who introduced Ramakrishna to the world at large. The result was that educated men from Calcutta, some of them to become his devoted disciples, went out to see him and listen to his conversation. These in due time were to carry Ramakrishna's message to the Western world.

During this period he talked almost incessantly. He wrote nothing, but his disciples took down his sayings. Because of his much speaking, a throat affection developed into cancer. He was taken to Calcutta, where he was attended by the best physicians. He still continued to talk on and on, until on March 15, 1886, he fell into a state of coma from which he never revived. After his death a group of his disciples decided to give their lives to the preaching of the doctrines of Ramakrishna.

According to Swami Vivekananda, his leading disciple, Ramakrishna made two diverse claims for himself. In his ordinary state he professed to be only the *servant* of all. But, as Vivekananda expresses it, "strange fits of God-consciousness came upon him," during which he claimed to be "eternally free and an incarnation [11] of God Himself"; in fact, the same soul that had been born before as Rama, as Krishna, as Buddha, and as Jesus.

How then shall we sum up the account of Ramakrishna? The living forces that were making a new India were pressing upon him. The world-wide propagation of Christianity was urging acceptance from Hindus, claiming to be the one religion for the whole world, and pressing its ethics upon all. There was also the growing power of Islam.

[11] It was the Brahmani nun who assured Gadadhar that he was, like Chaitanya, an incarnation of God. The thought thus planted in his ordinary consciousness reappeared in his more mystical states. Incarnation is not a difficult doctrine in Hinduism, since the whole universe, from one point of view, may be regarded as an embodiment of God. In fact, there are two views in Hinduism of the relation of the world to Ultimate Reality. The *exoteric* doctrine of emanation teaches that the world is an *apocalypse* disclosing a *Presence;* in other words, everything that exists is a manifestation of God. This is the theoretical basis of the populous pantheon of India, every one being permitted to make his own choice of what he will worship among the traditional 333,000,000 gods or beyond them. The *esoteric* doctrine of identity teaches that the world is a veil of unreality (Maya) hiding the face of the Ultimate Reality. This is the philosophical view as taught by Shankara, the waking world being regarded by him as no more real than the world of dreams.

Ramakrishna's doctrine of God and philosophy of religion represent his reaction to the religious situation. Just as all gods are relatively true as representatives of the One Absolute God, so all religions as sects are relatively true as representatives of, or paths to, the one Supreme Dharma or Absolute Religion. "Both Hindu and non-Hindu cults he harmonized on the basis of Hindu *Dharma.*[12] He thus sought to give to Vedantic Hinduism the things that belong to it, and to all religious cults, both Hindu and non-Hindu, including Islam and Christianity, the things that belong to them. If all religions are true, then, (1) every man should remain in the religion in which he was born; (2) no Hindu should abandon his religion in whole or in part; and therefore (3) everything in Hinduism should be defended. It all represents a "Counter-Reformation" against not only the foreign religions, Christianity and Islam, but also the reforming movements of India. With the winning of his disciples, Ramakrishna began to teach and thus to serve.[13] In his old capacity as priest of Kali he had neglected his duties and been a failure. There was no neglect now. With utter self-sacrifice he loved and served his disciples until the very end. He caught them with the cords of love and held them fast. It may be that his friendship with Keshab Chander Sen, that Hindu lover of Jesus Christ, gave him a new conception of love, service, and sacrifice.

[12] See *Hinduism Invades America* by Wendell Thomas, p. 62.
[13] See *op. cit.,* pp. 58-65.

CHAPTER VI

SWAMI VIVEKANANDA, INDIA'S APOSTLE TO THE WEST

It was about 1897 that I heard Vivekananda speak in Lahore, after his return from his triumphant visit to America. He was greeted everywhere in India as the great apostle and apologist of Hinduism. He spoke in English to a large audience. I was deeply impressed by his personality and message and went away from the meeting with a thrill and exaltation of spirit.

Narendra Nath Dutt was born in Calcutta, July 9, 1862, a member of the Kayasth, or writer caste. It is a remarkable coincidence that the first foreign missionary of modern Hinduism graduated from the General Assembly's Institution, a Christian Missionary College. He showed a keen interest in philosophy, and was remembered as a voracious reader, an imperious personality, and a vigorous debater. His ambition was to be, like his father, a great and wealthy lawyer.

His mother was the first religious influence in his life, a woman of character and intelligence, who could repeat large passages from the Hindu Epics. In his boyhood he showed fondness for wandering ascetics. While in college he learned about Jesus and the ethics of Christianity. Thus prepared, he came under the influence of Keshab Chander Sen, "the Christ-loving leader of the Brahmo Samaj";[1] and feeling an enthusiasm for social reform, he joined Keshab's society. But the Brahmo Samaj was only a half-way house for the young Narendra. In 1882 he met Ramakrishna the sage of Dakshineshwara, and though not impressed at first, soon came under his abiding influence. It was Keshab who had introduced Ramakrishna to the world, and, like John the Baptist, had pointed (perhaps unconsciously) his own disciple to one greater than he.

The sudden death of Narendra's father left the family in penury. Narendra's search for employment was unsuccessful. In great distress he turned to Ramakrishna and told his story. "Go," said the saint, "go to Mother Kali and pray." He prayed to Kali, and made a vow of renunciation. Several things combined to direct Narendra to the ascetic life. His grandfather had set an example. As a boy, Narendra had been fond of ascetics. The financial disaster that had overwhelmed the family, and especially the personal loss, had revealed the emptiness of life. And above all, there was the radiant example of Ramakrishna. From the first the Master gave his new disciple a great deal of attention. This spiritual nurture of a nature of great natural promise resulted, on the death of the Master in 1886, in Narendra Nath's becoming, under his new name Vivekananda, the

[1] *Hinduism Invades America* by Wendell Thomas, p. 66.

head of Ramakrishna's disciples and in time the founder of the Vedanta Society in America and the Ramakrishna Mission in India. He combined in himself the qualities of both Peter and John, being at once the administrative head and the intellectual and devotional leader of his fellow disciples.

The death of Ramakrishna was followed, according to the standard biographies, by vision and rapture and self-dedication. A group of disciples was walking in a garden one night and suddenly seemed to see a shining figure. It must be the Master. They were in quiet retreat at a little village, all sitting at night about a big fire, all meditating on the Master. Vivekananda opened his lips and told, as he remembered it from college days, the story of the Christ, and exhorted his brother disciples "to become themselves Christs, to aid in the redemption of the world." [2] The moment of rapture was also the moment of self-dedication. It suddenly dawned upon them that it was Christmas Eve!

The Parliament of Religions, held in Chicago in 1893, was the magnet that drew Swami Vivekananda to the West. He would go there and lift up his voice in defense of Hinduism. Against the missionary propaganda in the East he would launch a "counter-offensive" in the West. This, he said, was the meaning of his renunciation. His friends and admirers in South India provided funds, and he took with him a

[2] Quoted from Thomas' *Hinduism Invades America*, p. 70, as found in Virajananda, *Life of Swami Vivekananda*, Vol. II, p. 25.

stock of silk robes and colored turbans. He made an impression at the Parliament and elsewhere because of his fine command of English, readiness of speech, gorgeous apparel and genial personality. Above all he was a novelty,[3] the first Hindu many Americans had seen. And, withal, he delivered his message with conviction, with wise silence, it is true, on some points and considerable adjustment to American ears, but to the end that many people gained an entirely new conception of Hinduism. It is unnecessary to follow in detail the story of his triumphant progress through America. Everywhere he went, he was a guest. He was an especial favorite with the ladies. He expounded the Vedanta philosophy at numerous conferences, and was entertained by such people as Mrs. John J. Bagley, widow of the ex-Governor of Michigan, and the Hon. Thomas W. Palmer, formerly Senator and Minister to Spain. In 1894 he founded in New York City the Vedanta Society in America, and soon initiated Miss S. E. Waldo of Brooklyn as Sister Haridasi, Madame Marie Louise, a Frenchwoman, as Swami Abhayananda, and Leon Landsberg, a Russian Jew, as Swami Kripananda. These excessive labors meant weariness and compelled a rest, which he found on a sea voyage to England. It was there that he met and won to his allegiance Miss Margaret Noble, M.A., famous as "Sister Nivedita."

[3] I myself vividly remember seeing a native of India for the first time, in New York City in 1887. It was Dr. K. C. Chatterjee of Hoshiarpur.

What was Swami Vivekananda's impression of America? He found many friends and generous supporters, and felt that it was a most hopeful field for the preaching of the Hindu *Dharma*. He rejoiced that he had helped on the tide of Vedanta and foresaw the day almost at hand when the great majority of the West would follow it. But the Eastern ascetic found it hard to be a genuine Swami in America, and often longed to exchange his silken robes for the rags of an Indian monk, his sleep in the soft beds of America for sleep in India under the trees, and the queer food of the West (including *beef!*) for food secured in India by begging.

Early in 1896 he set out to return to India, stopping in England to strengthen the movement there. Before continuing his journey, he met Paul Deussen and Max Müller.[4] He was received with boundless enthusiasm in India as one who had preached Hinduism in the West and demonstrated its superiority to Christianity. He set to work at once, and in 1897 established the Ramakrishna Mission, a noteworthy institution which expresses the ideals of Buddhist and Christian service. Almost immediately on his return he was face to face with the great Indian famine of 1897-1899. He collected funds and administered relief. He opened one monastery after another, at Belur on the Ganges and at Mayavati in the Himalayas. He was interested in the education of

[4] Swami Vivekananda handed over to Prof. Max Müller some material on Ramakrishna, which was published in 1898 under the title, *Ramakrishna: His Life and Sayings.*

girls and women. In fact, he threw himself with all his might into service for India. Quite correctly does Wendell Thomas remark concerning him, that "if he was a Hindu to America, he was a Christian to India."

Again exhausted from overwork, and needing a change, as well as to see how his Western disciples were faring, he made the journey again to England and America. He went to Southern California, lectured in Pasadena and Los Angeles, found the people there especially open to the new teaching, and established several Vedanta centers on the Pacific Coast. Wearied with these strenuous efforts, he turned his face toward India, leaving America for the last time. He reached India more tired than when he left it, but continued to work. He founded a third monastery in Madras, and without lecturing did what he could to stir up people to labors of love and self-sacrifice. He had literally "burned to the socket," and the end was at hand. He died, July 4, 1902.

Such is a brief account of a very vigorous and influential personality. His addresses have been published in seven volumes. What are some of his ideas?

1. He rejoiced in the *comprehensiveness* of Hinduism: "From the high spiritual flights of the Vedanta philosophy . . . to the low ideas of idolatry with its multifarious mythology, the agnosticism of the Buddhists and the Atheism of the Jains, each and all have

a place in the Hindu's religion."[5] The implication is that Christianity and Islam might well find a place within the same system.

2. He defended *idolatry:* "When I have seen amongst them that are called idolaters, men, the like of whom in morality and spirituality and love I have never seen elsewhere, I stop and ask myself, 'Can sin beget holiness?'"[6] Clearly a reference to the practice of idolatry by his *guru,* Ramakrishna.

3. He declared that "there is no polytheism in India": "In every temple, if one stands by and listens, one will find the worshippers applying all the attributes of God, including omnipotence, to the *images.*" In one sense, it is true, there is no polytheism in India. Every name or image of a God in any age or country represents a human conception of the One Supreme Being. As in the case of the Vedic nature gods, any one of whom, by what Max Müller called the henotheistic attitude, could be worshipped as the Supreme God, so is it with the gods and images of modern India. In this sense as Dr. Justin Abbott points out, "Hindu theology is monotheistic."[7] But on the other hand, if there is no polytheism in India, then there is none in the whole world.

4. He held that "all religions are true." They are true, it may be admitted, in the sense that they are all the product of the religious nature of man working under diverse conditions of moral and spiritual

[5] *Works,* I, 4; compare Govinda Das, *Hinduism,* pp. 49-59.
[6] *Works,* I, 10.
[7] *A Garland of Hindu Prayers,* 1929, pp. xii-xiii.

insight. But they are not the same ethically any more than the gods of the world are ethically one and the same. This doubtless Vivekananda would have granted, for he declares that "to the Hindu the whole world of religions is only a travelling, a coming up, of different men and women, through various conditions and circumstances, to the same goal."[8] And again he says, "Be brave and sincere, then follow any path with devotion, and you must reach the Whole."[9] That is to say, "all religions are true" in the sense that they all lead to the same goal. In other departments of life, however, it is not subjective sincerity alone which counts, precious as that is, but objective truth.

5. He defined God in terms of *Love:* "God is the inexplicable, inexpressible essence of love. . . . Love is higher than works, than Yoga, than Knowledge. . . . Extreme love and highest knowledge[10] are one." Very good, and well put; but how is it to be reconciled with the statement, "The One must be without any qualities, even knowledge, and it cannot be the cause of the universe or of anything"?[11] If God, conceived as entirely separate from Maya, is without qualities such as knowledge and love, then the god who can be defined as love is within the sphere of Maya, and hence his love must be as illusory as his

[8] *Works,* I, 16.

[9] Virajananda, *Life of Swami Vivekananda,* Vol. II, p. 392, as quoted by Wendell Thomas, *Hinduism Invades America,* p. 88.

[10] *Works,* VII, 3, 7. Cf. *God is Love,* 1 John IV, 8, 16; Paul's Psalm of Love, 1 Cor. XIII; and Spinoza's *Amor Intellectualis Dei.*

[11] *Op. cit.,* VII, 54.

own separate existence. This emphasis on the Love of God looks like a contribution from Christianity, the fruit of Vivekananda's fellowship with Keshab Chander Sen, his studies in a Christian college, and his life in the West, but the real foundation of the Ramakrishna Mission is love for God and man.

6. He described creation as the *sport* of God: "The world is all for *play* and it amuses God; nothing in it can make God angry."[12] Then why should I be angry at the wrongs done in the world? It is clear that on this view the ethical is not a fundamental category. Again he says: "See good and evil as the *same,* both are merely God's play."[13] If good and evil are the same, then they are equal, the one to the other. Why then should I choose good rather than evil? This all looks like a heritage from the old Hindu metaphysics. Vivekananda's life was dominated more by the thought of the love of God. The metaphor, however, of creation as God's play fitly pictures creation as natural and as involving no effort on the part of God. Quite likely the original idea is a reflection of the natural and playful activity experienced in generation.

7. He was a Hindu apostle of the strenuous life. His ideal for men was that they should "work like lions."[14] Both his *guru,* Ramakrishna, and he himself, as teachers, richly fulfilled the ideal. They worked so hard, both of them, that their lives were

[12] *Op. cit.,* VII, 3.
[13] *Op. cit.,* VII, 11.
[14] *Op. cit.,* VII, 229.

cut short, Ramakrishna dying at fifty and Vivekananda at forty. It was on his first return from America that the great "social service" institution, the Ramakrishna Mission, was founded.[15] The impulse must have come largely from the West as the result of what Vivekananda had observed there of social responsibility issuing in social service.

8. He held the doctrine of *Maya,* or Cosmic Illusion. It is Shankara's doctrine of the superimposition of the object, which is mere appearance, upon the subject, which is reality.[16] Because of this the real unity is broken up into apparent multiplicity, even the multiplicity of souls being illusory. For all souls reduce to one Soul, as "the unity of all personalities,"[17] eternal and unchangeable. It is in this sense that the soul is equated with God. Or, to state the matter mythologically, "Kali, represented by a female figure standing with feet on a male figure, indicates that until *Maya* lifts, we can know nothing. . . . Brahman is neuter, unknown and unknowable, but to be objectified, covers Himself with a veil of Maya."[18] This is Shankara's doctrine of illusion, which Ramakrishna had learned from the naked ascetic Totapuri. The difference between good and evil is also illusory, since both are only "God's *play*"; or, differently stated: "Really, good and evil are one, and are in our own mind"; hence "we must find that

[15] See for a report of progress, *The Ramakrishna Math and Mission Convention, 1926.*

[16] *Works,* VII, 30.

[17] *Op. cit.,* VII, 16.

[18] *Op. cit.,* VII, 21.

we are beyond both evil and good." As means "to take away the veil, to lift off the bondage and illusion" Vivekananda prescribed "work and worship." [19]

9. He believed in Kali as "the Mother of the Universe." She is Brahman, when covered with the "veil of *Maya.*" She is "the Universal energy." She is the Kantian "time, space, and causation." "As conditioned, she is God, Nature, and Soul, the triangle of existence. . . . A bit of Mother, a drop, was Krishna, another was Buddha, another was Christ." [20] In all this we are reminded of Ramakrishna's priesthood in the temple of Kali at Dakshineshwara. The disciple, like the Master, championed the whole of Hinduism.

10. He graded the religiously creative personalities of history according to what seemed to him to be their importance: "As a character Buddha was the greatest the world has ever seen; next to him Christ." Thus "Buddha and Christ are the two biggest 'bubbles' the world has yet produced." In another place he mentions as "Great Incarnations of God–Krishna, Buddha, Jesus, and Rama Krishna." [21] Both Buddha and Christ, and all the rest from the point of view of the "higher knowledge," are "bubbles," and "every *worm* is the brother of the Nazarene." Nevertheless, confident of the future of mankind, Vivekananda foresees that "in time to come Christs will be in number like bunches of grapes on a vine." [22]

[19] *Op. cit.*, VII, 2, 51.

[20] *Op. cit.*, VII, 21, 25.

[21] *Op. cit.*, VII, 1, 5.

[22] *Op. cit.*, VII, 5.

11. He was haunted by the general idea of the Christian Trinity: "The Trinity—the knower, the known, and knowing—is manifested as this universe." Again "freedom, strength, sameness" are referred to as the Swami's trinity; and he speaks of "God, nature, and soul" as "the triangle of existence." [23]

12. He defined the soul in such a way as to teach the Godhead of man: "In its very essence, it is free, unbounded, holy, pure, and perfect." This is the key to the understanding of his words at the Parliament of Religions: "Ye holy and perfect beings, ye *divinities on earth*—sinners? It is a sin to call a man so." Such in his opinion is the soul as it really is, but not as it appears to be, for "somehow or other, it finds itself tied down to matter, and thinks of itself as matter" (the Vedanta doctrine of a "Fall"). In reality, however, "We are," as Vivekananda taught, "the greatest God that ever was or will be. . . . Bow down to nothing, but your own higher self. Your own will is all that answers prayer." [24]

13. He gave the primacy to mind: "Dis-identify yourself with the body and all pain will cease. This is the secret of healing." We are reminded of Christian Science.

14. He was the champion of fearlessness: "The greatest sin is to think yourself weak. No one is greater; realize you are Brahman. . . . The whole secret of existence is to have no fear. . . . Infinite

[23] *Op. cit.*, VII, 18, 25, 33.
[24] *Op. cit.*, I, 7, 9; VII, 76, 86.

strength is religion and God. . . . Fear is death. . . . Fearlessness is not possible as long as we have even God over us; we must be God."[25] This is Vivekananda's prescription against "slave-mentality."

15. He realized that mankind, empirically considered, needs to become better: "Do not say you are bad; say only you are good, but be better." From this point of view he rebuked his own countrymen for incontinence, child marriage and depriving women of their rights, for Brahman oppression of the low castes, and want of sympathy with the Pariahs, resulting in thousands of them "turning Christians," and for "laziness, meanness and hypocrisy."[26] Thus, like Mahatma Gandhi, Swami Vivekananda was an advocate of social reform.

16. He held that "consciousness is a bondage," that is to say, our ordinary consciousness, which belongs to the sphere of illusion. This is to be replaced by "super-conscious perception" (*samadhi*), through which God is realized. We are reminded of the trances of Ramakrishna. But so confident is Vivekananda of the spiritual evolution of the race that he writes: "What is now super-conscious for us will in ages to come be the conscious for all."[27]

17. He urged the necessity of being practical: "You have to be practical in all spheres of work. The whole country has been ruined by masses of the-

[25] *Works,* VII, 11, 45, 47, 52, 198. In the matter of fearlessness we may compare Swami Dayanand Sarasvati and Mahatma Gandhi.

[26] *Op. cit.,* VII, 20, 170-173, 180, 212-213, 216, 244.

[27] *Op. cit.,* VII, 37, 42.

ory." [28] We are reminded of Swami Ram's "Practical Vedanta."

Such are the doctrines which constituted the message of Swami Vivekananda to his own country and to the world. It is a wonderful mixture of ideas from widely different sources, popular Hinduism, philosophical Hinduism, Buddhism, Christianity, modern science, etc.—ideas not always consistent one with another, but preached with enthusiasm and conviction, and not infrequently shot through with gleams of insight.

[28] *Op. cit.*, VII, 133.

CHAPTER VII

SWAMI RAM TIRATH, THE POET-MONK OF THE PUNJAB

College student, professor of Mathematics, *sannyasi* and Himalayan ascetic, laughing philosopher of India, and advocate of "Practical Vedanta" in Japan and America—such was Tirath Ram [1] in various stages of his colorful career.

The chief events of his life may be briefly stated. He was born in 18 3 at Muraliwala, Punjab, of very poor Brahman parents; graduated from the Gujranwala High School and entered the Forman Christian College,[2] Lahore, 1888; married when quite young; B.A. from the F. C. College, 1892, and M.A. from the Government College, Lahore, 1893; professor of Mathematics, F. C. C., 1896; readership in the Ori-

1 His name Tirath Ram was changed on becoming a *sannyasi* to Swami Ram Tirath, or simply Swami Ram.

2 Three of Tirath Ram's teachers in the F. C. C., Lahore, bear witness concerning him. (1) "A mathematical prize man. Asked for a Revised Version of the Bible, and claimed to have been baptized with the Holy Ghost" (J. G. Gilbertson, Esq., M.A., May 2, 1931). (2) "A very attractive personality. Showed a deeply religious spirit and a mystical tendency. He told about some clairvoyant experiences, and his desire to follow what he considered divine leadings" (J. H. Orbison, M.D., Oct. 8, 1931). (3) "He was emotional and inclined towards mysticism. Everybody liked him, and he had great influence over the students. Many thought he would become a Christian" (Dr. H. C. Velte, Nov. 11, 1931).

ental College, Lahore, 1898; donned the yellow robe, 1901; visited Japan and America, 1902-1903; returned to India, 1904; drowned in the Ganges near Tehri, Garhwal, 1906, at the age of thirty-three.

Swami Vivekananda's visit to Lahore marked an epoch in Tirath Ram's life. The Bengali Swami's becoming an ascetic and preaching "practical Vedanta"—preaching it not only in the East, but also in Europe and America—fired Tirath Ram with an ambition to do the same things. Both were earnest men, in whose hearts burned the fire of Hindu religious zeal; both were graduates of Christian colleges; both exemplified stern renunciation; and both preached essentially the same doctrines. Thus in many respects Tirath Ram was simply a replica of Vivekananda. There were, however, differences. Vivekananda was unmarried when he donned the yellow robe, while the step involved for Tirath Ram the renunciation of wife and child. As a thinker and speaker, the Bengali Kayasth was superior to the Punjabi Brahman, but in poetic ecstasy and in the capacity for joy and laughter, Swami Ram was unique. These aspects of his personality came into view only after he had retired as a monk to the Himalayas, where he spent three years "on the naked bosom of nature." In the presence of the splendors and sublimities of this new environment Tirath Ram manifested the mood of a poet, being tremulously sensitive to the grandeur of mountains and the delicate beauty of flowers. Not infrequently "the effulgent glory" of things brought on "ecstasy and tears of joy."

Swami Ram's poems were largely the fruit of his experience in the Himalayas. While without the literary grace and perfection of Mrs. Naidu's work, they serve well as vehicles for his philosophy. Says Mr. C. F. Andrews: "I find in Swami Rama Tirath's poetic spirit, which lies behind his philosophy, the highest value of the written work." [3] Nature was for him a mirror in which the unity and spirituality and beauty of the "unseen universe," and the identity, as he conceived it, of all things with God, are disclosed. "He lives who can make of every object whatever a stepping-stone to God, or rather a mirror to see God. . . . The clouds dissolve, but leave a permanent message behind. They are only postmen. Miss not the Lord's love letter they have brought for you. . . . I myself am the pouring rain. I flash. I thunder. . . . All life is my God's life. The whole world is my Himalayan woods." [4] Or again:

> They say the sun is but His photo,
> They say that man is in His image,
> They say He twinkles in the stars,
> They say He smiles in fragrant flowers,
> They say He sings in nightingales,
> They say He breathes in cosmic air,
> They say He weeps in raining clouds,
> They say He sleeps in winter nights,

[3] *In Woods of God-Realization,* Vol. I, Introduction, p. liii.
[4] *The Story of Swami Ram Tirath* by Puran Singh, pp. 109-110, 113.

They say He runs in prattling streams,
They say He swings in rainbow arches.[5]

Again he sings:

Dear little violet, with the dewy eye,
Look up and tell me truly,
When no one is nigh
What thou art!

The violet answered with a gentle sigh,
If that is to be told when alone,
Then I must sadly own,
You will never know what am I,
For my brothers and sisters are all around,
In the air and on the ground,
And they are the same as I.[6]

This poetry is intended to clothe the philosophical thought that the core of reality–the truly real–in the violet as well as in all other things is God. Hence everything in the universe must, on these premises, be equated with everything else, and so the illusory multiplicity reduces to unity. Or, as Swami Ram sings in another place:[7]

The bodies are numerous, Soul is one,
That Soul supreme is none but I.
Free, free is every one to me,
No bondage, limit, fault I see.

[5] See *The Likeness of my Beloved,* in *Story,* p. 272. We are reminded of the "Hymn" at the close of Thomson's Seasons:
"These as they change, Almighty Father, these are but the varied God."

[6] *Story,* p. 273.

[7] *Story,* p. 266.

The freedom referred to is freedom from the veil of *Maya,* the Cosmic Illusion which, according to Shankara, converts the One into the many. Strip off the veil of ignorance, and both saint and sinner are the same, for both reduce to God. Swami Ram's chief disciple and biographer Puran Singh, tells how once Tirath Ram went to his old teacher, the late Dr. Sir James Ewing, Principal of the Forman Christian College, Lahore, and said: "You! you worship Christ! Have you seen Him with your eyes? No! You have not seen Him. Look! Look! Ewing!! Christ is standing before you." So Tirath Ram equated himself with Christ. In America he often saluted his hearers with the words, "My own Self in the form of ladies and gentlemen," or "the Infinite One in the form of ladies and gentlemen." On the premises of the Shankara Vedanta he could not but equate himself with equal truth and necessity with Nero, or any worst and vilest man, as well as with the best.[8]

The note that Swami Vivekananda sounded at Chicago, namely that of the Godhead of man, became the keynote of all of Swami Ram's utterances. This conviction is based upon the distinction drawn by both Swamis between the lower self and the Higher Self. The one is "satanic," and "mayavic." The other is the Highest Self, God. For both Swamis salvation consists in identifying oneself with God. "You are your own God," said Swami Ram. The

[8] Compare Mr. Gandhi's statement: "I cannot detach myself from the wickedest soul, nor may I be denied identity with the most virtuous," *Mahatma Gandhi's Ideas,* p. 305.

individual and lower selves are illusory and coalesce in their nothingness, since they are all equal to the same thing, that is, nothing.

The following verses also set forth the fundamental Vedantic antithesis between the One and the many, the Unchangeable and the changing, *Brahma* and *Maya:*

See, in this scene of changing shows
There is a changeless One that glows.
In seeming death, decay and pain,
It changes dress but comes again.
Love *that,* nor dress; love *Him,* not things.

. . . . .

The sky, the breeze, the river, rose,
Such veils of gauze for self He chose.
Hide as Thou mayst, I feel Thee;
Covers don't conceal but reveal Thee.
The forms are chased by one another,
That we may see the One they cover.

. . . . .

O Him I trust. Love Him I must,
The One in plurality, the only Reality. [9]

The meaning is clear. All the fleeing forms of nature are *mayavic,* illusory, unreal. And yet they are more than a veil to hide, they also *reveal.* In getting to know the hidden reality, mystical and poetic feeling has a part to play. The very purpose of nature is that we may penetrate to the Reality within and recognize the Unity disguised under the form of plurality.

[9] *Woods,* Vol. III, pp. 3-5.

Swami Ram was the Democritus, or "laughing philosopher," of modern India. His laughter was the expression of his joy. His poetry is lyric, the poetry of joy:

> O happy, happy, happy Ram!
> Serene and peaceful, tranquil, calm.
> My joy can nothing, nothing mar,
> My course can nothing, nothing bar.[10]

A poem of the laughing philosopher is *"I Cannot Suppress a Laughter."* The meaning is, in part, "What fools these mortals be!" to give all their attention to appearance and overlook *Reality*, but also in part it is a laughter of joy at his own discovery of reality and the identification of himself with it.

> The heart of everything I am,
> Instead of wish I gladness have.[11]

To illustrate the ways of the laughing philosopher, his biographer relates how at the Religious League at the St. Louis Exhibition, "he would laugh and laugh for minutes together in answer to some philosophical and theological questions, and say nothing in reply, as if his beaming, bubbling personality were enough reply to all the pretentious enquiries about man and God."[12]

His biographer tells us that he was a gloomy sort of child, fond of solitude.[13] In my recollection of Tirath Ram as a colleague I do not recall any mer-

[10] *Story*, p. 267.
[11] *Op. cit.*, pp. 263-264.
[12] *Op. cit.*, p. 4.
[13] *Op. cit.*, p. 63.

riment or laughter on his part, but rather seriousness. After he became a monk, he carried about with him "a miniature model of Krishna with flute in hand."[14] Was his hilarity the result of imitation of Krishna, or was it the effect of a profound psychological upheaval which transformed his early gloom into joy? No one knows the creative moment in his religious experience. Says his pupil-biographer: "He had realized life in its supreme beauty suddenly by some unknown personal touch that maddened him with a divine intoxication."[15] In his passionate devotion he reminds us of Chaitanya and the Bhakti saints of South India. In his love of the Himalayas and his ability to find spiritual lessons in nature he makes us think of Sadhu Sundar Singh.

Like Vivekananda, Ram Tirath emphasized love.

> I shall shower oceans of love;
> And bathe the world in joy.[16]

To Dr. H. C. Velte, his former teacher, he once said, "I love everybody." This note of love is hardly to be found in the Vedanta of Shankaracharya. It is clearly an expression of Hindu *bhakti* reinforced by Chris tianity.

Swami Ram taught a kind of neo-Vedanta, "Practical Vedanta," as he called it, which represented, as in the teaching of Vivekananda, a fusion of the strict *advaita* of Shankara with the altruism and philan-

[14] *Op. cit.*, p. 61.
[15] *Story*, p. 8.
[16] *Op. cit.*, p. 9.

thropy of Christianity. It was an attempt to trace out the implications of Shankara's doctrine of identity and illusion in such a way as to provide a program for individual and national progress. It was only toward the end of his career that Swami Ram began the study of Sanskrit—stung by the taunts of the Pundits of Benares and Allahabad that he did not know the sacred tongue; having previously spent four years in a Christian College, he was probably more intimately acquainted with Christian ethics than with Vedanta metaphysics. The Vedanta, as understood by him, was freely and poetically interpreted. Says his biographer: "Any good thing, any beautiful deed, any heroic action, when reported to him, elicited from him the remark, 'Ah! This is Vedanta.' Vedanta was a word that spelt everything noble, beautiful, spiritual and glorious in human history. It was no philosophy to him, it was all poetry." [17] And in another place his system is described as "No more a Vedanta than the prayer of a Muslim, or the devotion of a Bhagavata, or the fervour of a martyr, or the impulse of a patriotic hero, or the poetry of Shelley, or the philosophy of Spinoza, or the song of a woman in love." [18]

It is from this point of view that we can understand Swami Ram's message to America. Everything noble and worthy in American history and life was claimed as a fruit of Vedantic premises, albeit ignorantly held. Said he: "The saving element in Chris-

[17] *Story*, p. 278. [18] *Op. cit.*, p. 121.

tianity is Vedanta." As Paul declared to the Athenians the unknown object of their worship, so Swami Ram pointed out to the Americans the (to them) unknown sources of their individual and national well-being. Theirs was, however, only a partial Vedanta at the best. "America lives my Vedanta on the physical plane. Rama wants all nations to take the same truth on the mental and spiritual planes also. . . . Vedanta is the whole truth."

He felt the low estate of India. "India has shut herself from the spiritual, and has left only half a plank of her door open to the physical life, and her ruin has been complete on the mental plane." Why? "Because India lacks practical Vedanta."[19] Swami Ram's patriotism and "practical Vedanta" were combined as follows: "The land of India is my own body. . . . When I walk, I feel it is India walking; when I speak, India speaking; when I breathe, India breathing. I am India. . . . This is the highest realization of patriotism, and this is practical Vedanta. . . . Through *prana-pratishtha* Hindus endow with flesh and blood the effigy of Durga. Is it not worth while to evoke fire and life in the more real Durga of Mother India?"[20] Fired by patriotic zeal he made a prediction: "Whether working through many souls or alone, I seriously promise to infuse true life and dispel darkness and weakness from India within ten years; and within the first half of the twentieth cen-

[19] *Woods*, Vol. II, p. 117. [20] *Story*, pp. 232-233.

tury, India will be restored to more than its original glory." [21]

Nature may be viewed in two ways, as an apocalypse revealing a Presence, as in the well-known lines of Wordsworth, or as a veil hiding the mystery behind. The Vedic optimism is connected with the first conception, heaven and earth, sun and moon, thunder, lightning and rain, all revealing the indwelling Reality, God. Such was the view of Swami Ram in the days of his poetic exuberance and joy. Nature was to him "a mirror to see God." Every stick and stone, every tree, every animal and man revealed God. On this view the poetry of nature, as in the hymns of the Rigveda, becomes an expression of joy and a pæan of praise. So was it with Swami Ram until his "native hue" of poetic sensibility became "sicklied o'er with the pale cast of thought." For there is a second possible view of nature, namely that *it hides* rather than reveals. Swami Ram's own biographer feels that the fire ceased to burn in the Master, and his inspiration and power largely departed, when on his return from America he laid aside the weapons of mystical intuition and sought to equal the Pundits in the knowledge of Sanskrit and the methods of philosophical controversy. The scholastic system of Shankara was substituted for his own bright and poetic Vedanta. His native hue was sicklied over. And the result? Sadness. His life went out in

[21] *Woods,* Vol. I, front page.

gloom.[22] No one knows whether his drowning was by accident or through indifference.

Toward the close of his life Swami Ram said to his married disciple Puran Singh: "Rama never knew that this ochre garb is not of freedom. Slaves have begun to wear these robes.[23] . . . When Rama next goes down to the plains, in a full assembly, he will tear his robe into pieces in public and announce that the orange robe of the *Sannyasi* is no more a vehicle of freedom. . . . Rama is glad you have married. After all, a married life is a much stabler one."[24] He never went down again to the plains. New developments in his thought and life were cut short by death.

[22] *Story*, pp. 170-178, 281-291.

[23] Pundit Ganesh Dutt, long professor of Sanskrit in the Forman Christian College, Lahore, finally retired in order to spend his last days at Hardwar as a *sannyasi.* I was present when he said good-bye to his colleagues and old students. He left with colors flying. But within a few weeks he was back home again. The reason which he gave for the sudden reversal of his purpose was that he found few, or no, genuine ascetics at Hardwar. Slaves—and even worse—knaves, were wearing the yellow robe.

[24] *Story*, pp. 277-278.

CHAPTER VIII

JIDDU KRISHNAMURTI, MRS. BESANT'S WORLD-TEACHER

MRS. ANNIE BESANT had a most dramatic career, rebounding from orthodox Christianity to Bradlaugh's secularism, and finally discovering in Theosophy the synthesis of the two extremes. She was born in London, in 1847, of an Irish family in which "belief in 'ghosts' of all descriptions was general." Like her future preceptress, Madame Blavatsky, she had a "faculty for seeing visions and dreaming dreams." [1] Her father was a skeptic, her mother a devout Episcopalian, and her other relatives Roman Catholics. In her autobiography Mrs. Besant writes (p. 24): "The Roman Catholic Church, had it captured me as it nearly did, would have sent me on some mission of danger and sacrifice and utilized me as a martyr." Once in Lahore, India, Principal George Adam Smith predicted in my hearing that Mrs. Besant would finally land in the Roman Church. This prophecy has been in a sense fulfilled by the formation of the Liberal Catholic Church as a Theosophic appanage with Mr. Leadbeater as Bishop and Mrs.

[1] *Annie Besant; an Autobiography* by Dr. Annie Besant, London, 1908, pp. 25, 27.

Besant presumably a member "in good and regular standing."

In 1866 Annie Wood met Rev. Frank Besant, an Episcopal clergyman, idealized him and married him. It was a short-lived experiment. For some time she had been beset with doubt and finally her doubts conquered. She gave up Christianity, and left her home and her husband (though retaining his name), finding refuge in the camp of Secularism. Here she remained for fifteen years (1874-1889), atheistic in religion, utilitarian in ethics, and radical in politics. In the place of God she put inexorable Law. In association with Mr. Bradlaugh she found abundant opportunities to exercise her gifts as a public speaker.

Meanwhile she was pursuing studies in dreams, hallucinations and spiritualistic phenomena, and had read Sinnett's *Occult World*. As a result she was convinced of the existence of some "hidden power" in the universe and resolved to find it. In 1888 W. T. Stead asked her to review Madame Blavatsky's *Secret Doctrine*. It was enough. She became a disciple of "H. P. B."

The Theosophical Society was founded in 1875 in New York City by Helena Petrovna Blavatsky, Col. Olcott, and some fourteen others. Soon, however, "the Theosophical twins," Blavatsky and Olcott, shook off the dust of their feet against America and went to India, that ancient home of the occult. There, in order to win disciples as well as to earn their bread, various manifestations of (what seemed to be) the occult were displayed by them. It is a highly controversial subject, but, to put the matter gently, at least some of their manifestations were shown, with practical certainty, to be fraudulent. Notably so in the case of the Madras exposure in 1884, which the British Society of Psychical Research investigated through their agent Richard Hodgson, and as a result pronounced Madame Blavatsky a charlatan.

Mrs. Besant is clearly "H. P. B.'s" most famous convert. James, the psychologist, referred to her as "that high-souled woman." In September, 1933, she died at the age of eighty-six, and throughout her long years of residence in India she has been conspicuous. Some thirty years ago I heard Mrs. Besant address an audience of Hindus in Lahore. Her words were those of a reformer, direct and trenchant. She appealed to the Hindu community to set its house in order. Her words of criticism against unworthy Hindu ways aroused no resentment, since Mrs. Besant through her love for and self-identification with India had won the right to speak plainly, as Katherine Mayo had not.

During her forty years in India Mrs. Besant was a lecturer, writer, educationalist, and occultist. Through lectures she expounded and defended Hinduism, Theosophy, taking over from Hinduism the doctrines of transmigration and karma and many other things besides. Like Madame Blavatsky, Mrs. Besant was a most prolific writer, some sixty titles of books and pamphlets being listed under her name.[2] In 1898 Mrs. Besant helped in the foundation of the Central Hindu College, Benares, and served for some time on its Governing Board.

The program of Theosophy is universalistic. Members of all religions are invited to join the Theosophical camp, no one having to renounce his old religious connection. In fact the new affiliation is referred to as a means of helping the old. In Lahore an Indian Christian once suggested to me that we both become members of the local Theosophical Lodge.

Theosophy appeals to Hindus because almost everything in Hinduism is defended by Theosophy. A friendly gesture is held out to Buddhism through the initiation into Buddhism of "H. P. B." and Col. Olcott and through the location of the Masters in Tibet. An appeal is made to Christianity through assertions of its esoteric character and through the founding of the Liberal Catholic Church with an ornate ritual and with Bishops, who claim to be in the line of "Apostolic succession." [3]

Theosophy has its philosophy of religion, namely that religions never evolve, but always degenerate. It is a doctrine of "primitive revelation," the ancient wisdom being the gift to humanity of perfected World-Teachers. As such, like Pallas springing full-armed from the brain of Zeus, it is originally com-

2 See Kuhn's *Theosophy*, pp. 355-358.
3 See *Is Theosophy Anti-Christian?* by Mrs. Besant, 1904.

plete. As a result, however, of the process of degeneration present-day religions exhibit only the *disjuncta membra* of what at the beginning were "profound and coherent systems."[4] Theosophy attempts to "reconstruct the scattered remnants." It thus claims to be the vital essence of all religions.

Theosophists in general believe in the existence of "the Great White Brotherhood" of perfected men, who are said to live in the flesh somewhere in the recesses of Tibet. It is claimed that they are able to send messages of guidance and inspiration to those qualified to receive them. This is perhaps the most controversial doctrine of Theosophy, not even all Theosophists accepting it. Most of the exposures and schisms which have befallen the cult have been connected with the alleged messages from the Masters.[5] The author of *The Mysterious Madame* traces a development in "H. P. B.'s" controls, "John King" for the West, "the Brothers of Luxor" for Egypt, and the Mahatmas of Tibet, when "H. P. B." reached India in 1879, the inference suggested being that all alike are products of the imagination.

After the death of Madame Blavatsky, the most notable development was that of Neo-Theosophy under the direction of Mrs. Besant and Mr. Leadbeater. It included within its program the Liberal Catholic Church as a Theosophical adjunct, the Order of the Star in the East as a preparation for the coming World-Teacher, and the identification of the

[4] Kuhn, *Theosophy*, p. 4. [5] *Op. cit.*, p. 316.

World-Teacher in the person of Jiddu Krishnamurti.

Krishnamurti, son of a Madrasi Brahman, was placed by his father under the charge of Mrs. Besant to be educated, and she in turn left him largely to the care of Mr. Leadbeater. But Mr. Leadbeater had been accused of holding questionable theories, if not of open immorality. Naturally the father raised objections, and the matter was carried to the courts. On the basis of a psychic discovery claimed by Mr. Leadbeater in 1908, Jiddu Krishnamurti was regarded by Mrs. Besant as the one whose body is to be "a vehicle for the World-Teacher." The Coming One would be called Christ [6] by Christians, Bodhisattva or Maitreya by Buddhists, and Krishna by Hindus. It was "a master-stroke to capture at once Christianity, Buddhism, and Hinduism for the Theosophical Society." [7] To honor further the Hindu lad, who had such a heavy burden of dignity to support, Mr. Leadbeater published *The Lives of Alcyone*, a unique kind of genealogy based upon alleged clairvoyant investigation, in which no less than forty different reincarnations of Krishnamurti are described in detail. Thus Mrs. Besant and Mr. Leadbeater worked together as the later "Theosophical twins," very much as did the earlier twins, "H. P. B." and Col. Olcott. In both cases the man was the henchman of the woman.

How did Krishnamurti play his part in the drama

[6] Compare "the Promised Messiah" of the Ahmadiya movement in the Punjab.

[7] Farquhar, *Modern Religious Movements*, p. 274.

prescribed? He had studied at Oxford, and his English is good though diffuse. He is also rather slow of speech, but from all accounts is on the whole an attractive figure. Seven international camps have been held in Ommen, Holland, in connection with the Order of the Star. In 1925 Krishnamurti selected seven out of twelve proposed Apostles. He has visited America at least four times—in 1926, 1928, 1929, and 1931. He has published several pamphlets which contain his testimony concerning himself. In one of them he begins with a vision of his Happiness, his Guru, his Beloved. His beloved is defined as "himself, ennobled, glorified, made perfect." [8] The consequence is intense happiness, and the desire to share with others. "Now that I feel I am one with the Beloved, I can say, 'I am the World-Teacher,' [9] a thing which I could not say before." Now follow enormous claims, which, summed up, amount to the assertion that he has reached a certain altitude above ordinary human beings; has attained to liberation and the Kingdom of Happiness; is conscious of being "Truth" and "Life"; possesses in full measure the fountain of the waters of life; is the Standard for the world and the end of all search; therefore in very truth the World-Teacher [10] belonging to the succession of those who have attained.

Such is Jiddu Krishnamurti's testimony concerning himself. But in 1929 he dissolved the Order of

[8] *Pool*, p. 24; *Authority*, p. 66.
[9] *Truth*, p. 45.
[10] *Authority*, pp. 68 69, 85; *Understanding*, pp. 27, 89.

the Star, retaining for himself only the obscure rôle of a spiritual teacher. He evidently found the exalted position which had been assigned him uncomfortable to support. In view of the great aberrations of Neo-Theosophy and especially of the Alcyone Cult, it is probable that not a few Theosophists agree with Mrs. Cleather in the characterization of Mrs. Besant as the "evil genius" of the Theosophical Society.

More recently Krishnamurti has renounced his affiliation with the Theosophical Society entirely and has established himself in California in the modest rôle of an independent religious teacher.

CHAPTER IX

SHIV NARAYAN AGNIHOTRI AND "SCIENCE-GROUNDED RELIGION"

An old man of about eighty years, head of a Hindu sect which dethrones God and elevates its founder to the vacant place, creator of a so-called "science-grounded religion" which regards all other religions as "fiction-grounded"—such is Pundit S. N. Agnihotri, head of the Deva Samaj, Lahore. His story illustrates how the currents of modern thought play with transforming power upon the life of even a Brahman of the Brahmans.

Shiv Narayan Agnihotri was born in 1850 in the village of Akbarpur, not far from Cawnpore, India. He came of a distinguished Agnihotri family of Kanyakubja Brahmans. His great grandfather Pundit Ganga Parsad Agnihotri was Dewan of Akorhi state; his grandfather, Ram Jivan Agnihotri, led a very saintly life; his father Rameshwar Agnihotri was a strict vegetarian and teetotaller, and his mother, the daughter of an Indian officer in the British Army, was a lady of strong will power and deep religious faith. The religion of his home was probably Shaiva orthodoxy of a popular type, like that of his later antagonist Swami Dayanand Sarasvati. In all of his kaleidoscopic changes in thought and practice he retained up to his death at least a few things which marked his early home life, namely, the practice of *ahinsa,* the non-killing of any sentient being, and the practice of vegetarianism and total abstinence from intoxicating liquors ("barring certain right occasions" in all these cases); but, most important of all, he had retained to the end the typically Brahman superiority complex, which prompted him to say even in the days of his religious apprenticeship that he was born to rule, not to obey.

While a student all his life, his preliminary education was defective. To be sure, he knew English, but he had apparently little knowledge of Sanskrit, although he was a Brahman. At the age of sixteen he entered the Government Engineering College at Rurki. He finished the "overseer" course in two years, after which he held various posts up to 1873 when he accepted the position of drawing master in the Government School, Lahore. We may note in his early education the dominance of mathematical and mechanical studies and the absence of more widely cultural studies in literature and philosophy. But religious creativeness in India is known to coexist at times with intense preoccupation in mathematical studies, as in the case, for example, of Swami Ram Tirath.

The early spiritual pilgrimage of Agnihotri begins at Rurki, where he manifested for a time certain ascetic tendencies which alarmed his wife Lilavati, to whom he had been betrothed at the age of eleven. Rurki, too, marked the beginning of his interest in social reform, and the banishment of the purda from his home. The most important spiritual event of the Rurki period, however, was the influence over both him and his wife of P. Shiv Dayal Singh, curator of the College, who taught them the Vedanta doctrine of the identity of the individual soul with the Universal Soul and in 1871 initiated them as disciples. This represents the Vedanta period in the life of Pundit Agnihotri, but this, as also a similar experience in the life of Swami Dayanand Sarasvati, was only a passing phase.

At Lahore, in 1873, Pundit Agnihotri came under the influence of the Brahmo Samaj through discussions with a Brahmo pundit who taught him Sanskrit. He found himself in sympathy with the Brahmo program of social reform, so that before long both he and his wife deserted the Vedanta conception of God as impersonal, and accepted the Brahmo view that God is personal. His rise in the Brahmo Church was rapid. Successively he was made honorary minister of the Lahore Samaj (1875-1882) and a regular full-time preacher (1882-1887). He was ordained at Calcutta (1880) as one of the first missionaries of the *Sadharan Brahmo Samaj,* and became a Brahmo *Sannyasi,* thereby realizing the tendency displayed at Rurki toward the ascetic life. In imitation of Salvation Army methods he established a Brahmo Army. Always an eloquent and magnetic speaker, during this period he wielded a large influence in Lahore in all matters of social reform.

But gradually the entering wedge of friction began to divide Pundit Agnihotri from his fellow Brahmos. He felt that he was born to rule. Indeed, he was a natural leader of men. People had hung upon his eloquence, a circumstance not ordinarily making for humility. The Brahmos naturally became apprehensive lest he should declare himself a Guru. They did not approve his adoption of Salvation Army methods. The result was Agnihotri's secession from the Brahmo Samaj on the Queen's Jubilee Day (February 16, 1887), and the subsequent organization of the Deva Samaj. Though the immediate grounds of the breach were not doctrinal, doctrinal differences of great significance soon emerged. The creed remained in its major outlines as before, but with significant differences. Following the example of the great Keshab Chander Sen, Agnihotri declared that the Deva Dharma or Divine Religion was "a special divine dispensation," and of course he himself was its special Guru and Prophet. The Guru-doctrine grew apace. By October, 1892, Agnihotri was able to say, "My mission is unique. . . . I am free from sin. . . . I am a ship of hope for elevating nations."

When Pundit Agnihotri left the Brahmo Samaj, in order to have a distinctive name for his religion he substituted the old Vedic word *Deva* (God) in place of the Upanishad word *Brahma* (God), thereby getting the name *Deva Samaj* instead of Brahmo Samaj.

The name for God in the theistic period of the Deva Samaj was *Paramadeva,* i.e., Highest Deva. But sinful men through conversion may obtain *nava jivan* (new life), and progressively *Deva jivan* (divine life). Hence such people, as "partakers of the divine nature," may receive a new name compounded of *Deva,* if men, and of *Devi,* if women. Ram Jawahir Mull received the new name Mangal Dev, and a Hindu lady the new name Prem Devi. Thus while there is only one *Paramadeva* in the older theology of the Deva Samaj, there are many *devas* and *devis.* The universal church of the future was to be known as the *Deva Raj,* or "kingdom of God."

Like the Brahmo Samaj, the Deva Samaj in its theistic form claimed a universal mission. It was a special Divine Dispensation for mankind. Caste was rejected as "injurious and sinful," and the door was open for every man and woman from any caste and nation to enter the Deva Samaj on equal terms.

The creed of the theistic Deva Samaj, like the creeds of the Brahmo Samaj and the Arya Samaj, consists of ten articles. It is an answer to the question, What do the Deva Dharmis believe? As a theological creed, it has doctrines of God, of man, of salvation, and of holy scripture. God is a *personal* God, called, after the Brahmo fashion and general Hindu style, both Father and Mother. Man is declared to be immortal, natural inherent immortality apparently being meant, and transmigration, as we know from other sources, is rejected. The sinfulness of man is assumed throughout the creed and the necessity of liberation from sin, of conversion from sin, is strongly emphasized. Man's freedom to receive "new life," "the life of God," "the power of God," is an implicit postulate. Thus the older theology of the Deva Samaj asserts the reality of God, Freedom, and Immortality. Salvation (*mukti*) is defined as "liberation from sin," not as deliverance from repeated births. No more than the Brahmo Samaj did the theistic Deva Samaj "confine divine truths and spiritual teachings exclusively to any particular book or spiritual teacher," but, positively, made the Deva Dharma revelation the standard of all religious truth, for all other religious teachings are true only *so far as they coincide with the ideal and teachings of the Deva Dharma.* This is practically as high a doctrine of revelation as held by Christian or Muslim. In the official creed of the theistic Deva Samaj the doctrine of the *Deva Guru,* or "Divine Teacher" (the standing title of Pundit Agnihotri), while implicit and disguised, can readily be made explicit. The teachings of the Deva Dharma religion, both oral and written, emanate from the Deva Guru, and they are declared to be divine revelation, the test and standard of all religious truth. The Deva Dharma is the creation of the Deva Guru, and "sinners can get new life upon the conditions prescribed by the Deva Dharma," which is declared to be "a special Divine Dispensation for mankind." Similar claims, more explicitly stated, are found in the literature of the early period. In the *Dharma Jivan,* October 4, 1892, the Deva Guru writes concerning himself (in the third person) that "he and his mission are not two things, but one; he is the special manifestation and example of the life of holiness." The doctrine of the Deva Guru in the theistic Deva Dharma is thus a high one. The Deva Guru is a person of universal significance, because he is the founder of the absolute religion, the author of a scripture which is the test of truth in all other scriptures, and the supreme manifestation of the life of holiness.

The boundary between the Deva Guru's old theology and new was fixed by the libel case, *Chanda Singh versus S. N. Agnihotri*, which dragged itself out through five years (1893-1898). One interesting thing in connection with the case was the vivid impression made upon Gurmukh Singh, the counsel of Agnihotri's opponent, by the earnestness of the Deva Samaj people and by their good deportment. Before long Gurmukh Singh openly joined the Deva Samaj and became their leader in Ferozepore. These five years were marked not only externally by the vexatious legal case, but also internally by a thoroughgoing examination of the foundations of the theistic Deva Samaj which soon caused all public preaching and controversy to stop, as well as all publication of books and papers. Indeed as far as possible all the literature of the theistic Deva Samaj was withdrawn from circulation. The Deva Guru went into the silence as a theist, but emerged as an atheist!

Five stages, then, may be distinguished in the spiritual pilgrimage of Agnihotri: first, popular Hinduism (Akbarpur); second, Vedantism (Rurki); and the last three at Lahore, namely, the Brahmo Samaj, the theistic Deva Samaj (1887-1893), and the atheistic Deva Samaj to 1929, when Agnihotri died.

The terminology of the theistic Deva Samaj was largely retained in the last and atheistic stage. The society was still the *Deva Samaj,* the "Divine Society," and the founder was still the *Deva Guru,* the "Divine Teacher." But a new creed and a new set of principles, strikingly different from the old, were framed. The theological decalogue of the theistic society was replaced by an *ethical* decalogue.[1] If the former tells what the theistic Devadharmis believed, the latter tells what the atheistic Devadharmis vow to *do.* The ethical decalogue is in the form of ten negative commandments prohibiting bribery, theft, false witness, dishonesty, gambling, idleness, adultery and kindred sins, use of intoxicants, flesh-eating and the killing of any sentient being. The candidate for membership vows to avoid all of these things. As in the case of Gautama Buddha, himself an Indian of the Indians, the passing of the metaphysical was accompanied by a compensatory ethical emphasis. One would like to know the whole history of the Deva Guru's momentous shift from theism to

[1] It was (I think) in 1898 that I called on Pundit S. N. Agnihotri. He received me kindly and in our conversation stressed the importance of the ethical. One or more of his sons have been students in the Forman Christian College, Lahore.

atheism. Perhaps, like Buddha, he was convinced that many social evils in his own country and throughout the world are buttressed by religion. He knew, too, that India is profoundly religious, and certainly not atheistic, and so he must have been aware of the very great risk involved in the change. No wonder it took half a decade or more for him to makc the great decision. That he did make it and came forth boldly as an atheist in the face of the massed opposition that he knew he would meet, attests his integrity of spirit. India has had at least two types of atheism, the *Charvaka* type, which is materialistic, hedonistic and dogmatic, and the Buddhist type, which is agnostic and ethical. The atheism of the Deva Guru is ethical, like that of Buddha, but dogmatic, like that of the Charvakas. Further comparing the atheistic Deva Samaj with Buddhism, we note that in both cases there is an *atheistic* society with a *moral* program, and that before long in both cases the founder himself became practically God.

If the first stage in the religious position of S. N. Agnihotri was determined by the traditions and beliefs of popular Hinduism, the second by the metaphysical principles of Shankaracharya, and the third and fourth by the teachings of the Brahmo Samaj, the fifth was dominated by the concepts of modern science. It is obvious that the nature of his early training at Rurki and the work he followed at Lahore as a drawing master predisposed his mind somewhat narrowly to the points of view of science. There is evidence also that he had read Spencer's *First Principles* and other works of the English empirical and evolutionary schools. In the later literature of the Samaj there are numerous references to nature, law, matter, force, seed, soil, growth, life-force, evolution, degeneration, extinction, etc. Matter and force are declared to be uncreated and indestructible. They are the constituents of the universe and exist in four forms: inorganic, vegetable, animal, human. Since matter and force are the only reality, there is no such thing as God or gods. Men have to do, not with a personal god, an inheritance from "the days of ignorance," but with an impersonal law, the Law of Evolution and Dissolution.[2] Living seeds, if sown at the proper time and in the proper soil, will evolve and live; otherwise they will dissolve and die. The life of a man is a living seed which if planted in the Deva Samaj as a garden will then and only then evolve and bear fruit, for outside of the Deva Samaj there is no possibility of escape from the forces of dissolution. The Deva Samaj alone is the science-grounded religion because based on the two principles, evolution and dissolution. All other religions without exception are fiction-grounded. The end of evolution is life beyond the grave, but the end of dissolution is the death of both body and spirit.

[2] In this substitution of an impersonal law for a personal God the "new theology" of the Deva Guru shows affinities with Buddhism and Theosophy as well as with the positivistic system of Comte.

The Deva Guru, according to the doctrine, is the supreme result of the evolutionary process up to date, and so possesses the powers of the Complete Higher Life, not only having life in himself, but also being able to give it to others. A book that profoundly influenced the thought of Pundit Agnihotri was Henry Drummond's *Natural Law in the Spiritual World.* The chapter on Biogenesis begins with the quotation, "He that hath the Son hath life, and he that hath not the Son of God hath not life" (1 John V, 12). The analogous doctrine of the Deva Samaj is: He that hath the Deva Guru hath life and he that hath not the Deva Guru hath not life. In place, then, of natural immortality is the conditional immortality of the Deva Guru's "new theology." Spiritual contact with the Deva Guru as a life-giver is the condition of attaining to the complete higher life, which is raised above the danger of degeneration and extinction. The Deva Samaj doctrine of conditional immortality is not unlike that preached in London by the Reverend Edward White shortly before the rise of the Deva Samaj.

The Deva Guru does not claim to be a supernatural personage. His place is under the law of Evolution, but—and this indicates his dignity—his place during his own generation is the *highest* place under that law. He represents up to the present time the supreme product of evolution. That is, he has reached a point, intellectually, morally, and spiritually, which no other man has ever reached. He occupies a unique position and has in all things pre-eminence. He is the consummate fruit of the religious spirit. As such he is the true religious leader for all mankind, declared so not by the decrees of men, but by the infallible indications of the evolutionary process. Did Pundit Agnihotri regard himself as in any sense an incarnation? Not in the popular sense, but he did apparently regard himself as the highest concrete embodiment that had then appeared of that fulness of light and power, of life and law, which seems to constitute the ultimate reality of all things.

In harmony with the above characterizations are the titles given to the Deva Guru (doubtless with his own consent), such as "the One True Worshipful Being for all Mankind. . . . Most Exalted, Divine Teacher, Blessed Lord . . . *Sattya Deva* (True God), and *Deva Atma* (Divine Spirit)." The Deva Guru is clearly conceived by himself and by his followers as God (or the equivalent of God) manifested in the evolutionary process.

Spiritual contact with the Deva Guru as a life-giver is the condition of attaining to the complete higher life, which is raised above the danger of degeneration and extinction. We have here the "doctrine of the survival value of moral goodness." Those that are able to transcend death exist in the form of a refined human body, that is, a kind of spiritual body. This is akin to the old Vedic view as well as to the Christian view. There is no return from the other world. The soul is defined as "man's life-force," and the pre-existence of the soul is denied. The Deva Guru in his later years taught and practiced Spiritualism. He is said to have had personal dealings with the souls of the departed, many of his own dead relatives having found salvation through him. Thus he delivered addresses to spirits who assembled from time to time to hear him at the Samaj building. He was clearly influenced by the writings of such scientists as Sir Oliver Lodge, Sir William Crooke, and Dr. Alfred Russell Wallace, for he writes: "The fact that many souls do survive after death is being established by Western Spiritualism." [3]

The doctrine of Karma is held only in the form that good action leads to development and evil action to degeneration, the process in both cases being automatic. But the tendency to evil action can be stayed by union with the Deva Guru, and good action can thereby be stimulated. This is very different from the orthodox doctrine of Karma, and amounts to its rejection. The closest philosophical affinity of the later Deva Samaj is with the Sankhya, but there are wide differences. According to the Sankhya, deliverance is the emancipation of the soul from *prakriti* (matter), and takes place through "discriminating knowledge" (an *intellectual* process) by virtue of which one discerns the absolute difference between spirit and matter. But according to the Deva Samaj deliverance is emancipation from evil habit (an *ethical* process), and takes place through the recognition

[3] *Science-Grounded Religion,* May 1923, p. 13.

of the Deva Guru as the possessor of complete higher life and through union with him by faith and surrender.

Since the person of the Deva Guru is unique, everything connected with him is also declared to be unique: unique light, unique power, unique teachings, unique society. There is no doctrine here that "all religions are true." "The Deva Atma, the only true worshipful being for mankind," stands over against all lesser lights, the "one science-grounded religion" stands opposed to the many fiction-grounded religions. Thus the Deva Samaj doctrine of the Deva Guru is as uncompromising as the Christian doctrine of the Lord Jesus Christ.

A fair number of disciples followed the Deva Guru into the atheistic Samaj. Some went into one or other of the reforming sects, others embraced Christianity, and others went back into orthodox Hinduism. In order to become a member of Deva Samaj, the candidate writes a letter to the Deva Guru, giving a catalogue of past sins and promising to give them up, and explaining how he was brought through the teachings of the Deva Guru to a better state of mind. These documents are carefully filed. They constitute a kind of recorded confessional. A threefold pledge is exacted of a member: to abstain from the ten sins mentioned in the "ethical decalogue"; to refrain from false belief in so called worshipful beings; and positively to have faith in the Deva Atma as the "highest worshipful being." This represents an attempt to secure quality rather than quantity in the membership. A few thousand members are reported. The chief source of the membership is probably Sikhism and the chief centers are Lahore and Ferozepore.

Since the Deva Guru became virtually the god of the Deva Samaj, he practically withdrew from all public activities, and confined his ministry to his disciples. Hence the Samaj has become a semi-secret religious society. Its devotional meetings are private. The portrait of the Deva Guru on such occasions is garlanded with flowers, a hymn is sung in his praise, and all prostrate themselves before the portrait of Agnihotri as the *Sattya Deva* or True God.

Two measures of the Deva Guru in 1913 raised a storm in the Samaj. The first was the appointment of his son Devanand as his successor. Pundit Dev Ratan, who had been his secretary and right hand man for twenty-four years, did not approve the appointment, perhaps having hoped to be appointed himself. The second was the publication of a book in which the Deva Guru declared himself to be the perfect ideal, the perfect object of worship, the perfect giver of life. No one has been equal to him in the past, and no one will ever equal him in the future. Which means, in other words, that the evolutionary process has exhausted itself in the production of S. N. Agnihotri.

The consequence was the secession of Dev Ratan, besides one of the sons of the Deva Guru, his brother-in-law, his sister-in-law, and some others. But the bulk of the members remained. The seceders formed "The Society for the Promotion of Higher Life," holding to the old teaching, without the Deva Guru. The letters of confession written by Dev Ratan in former years have been published by the Deva Guru to show what a bad man he was.[4]

In 1917, a Constitution for the Deva Samaj was prepared. There is a Council and a Representative Assembly, and voters must possess certain qualifications. The whole is "under the guidance of the Founder-President."

The strong point in the Deva Samaj is its emphasis on the *ethical* in both individual and social life. For the individual there is need of repentance, confession, restitution, and amendment. I recall the last Deva Samaj public meeting I attended in Lahore. Quotations from letters were read (without names of course) which detailed the sins into which the writers had fallen and their deliverance through the teaching of the Deva Guru. It was a kind of Deva Samaj "testimony meeting." The social-reform activities enumerated for 1923 were: four schools for the depressed classes; two settlements of criminal tribes; an inter-caste dinner for social unification; and the definition of "gross sins" in the ethical decalogue. The

[4] I recall some controversial correspondence with P. Dev Ratan in the early days. The last time I met him was at the Kumbh Mela in Allahabad, 1918, when he was the secretary and assistant of Dr. Kurtkoti, who officiated at the wedding ceremony of the Ex-Maharaja of Indore and Nancy Miller of Seattle, Washington.

Samaj has brought about some cases of widow remarriage, and intercaste marriage, and has worked steadily against the early marriage of children, sale of daughters to old men, polygamy, and extravagance in marriage. Some eighteen widows have become teachers, "being saved from their degraded condition," and disputes, as a rule, have been settled within the Samaj instead of in Government Courts.

There are numerous coincidences between the Deva Samaj conception of the Deva Guru and the Christian conception of Jesus Christ. Both are represented as deliverers from sin, a grim anthropological background of moral bondage being postulated in both systems. Both deliverers are conceived as gifts; the one, the gift of God, and the other, the gift of the evolutionary process. Both deliverers are regarded as unique; the one being "the only name given under heaven, whereby we must be saved," and the other being "the one true worshipful being for all mankind." Saving contact with each is made through faith, confession of sin, surrender, and obedience. Each claims to be sinless, and so able to deal adequately with sin. Each claims to possess the powers of the higher life which are able to overcome death. Each claims the ability to open the gates of the future life to true believers. Each in his message puts the emphasis upon repentance, confession, restitution, and amendment. And both are objects of worship for their followers.

One wonders whether Pundit Agnihotri had not

made the life of Christ an object of serious study. He was introduced to Christian ideas through the reading of English books, through the principles of the Brahmo Samaj, through the work of Major Booth-Tucker of the Salvation Army, and through that of Christian missions going on for long years in Lahore. He may have desired to raise a bulwark against the spread of Christianity in India by giving to the people in himself a kind of Hindu Christ. Or, seeing the ethical fruits of the religion of Jesus, he may have earnestly desired to inaugurate the same kind of movement, but based upon what, according to his view, are sounder foundations. At any rate, however we may explain it, there appears in the life of S. N. Agnihotri and in his society a real ethical enthusiasm.

CHAPTER X

SWAMI DAYANAND SARASVATI AND THE WATCHWORD "BACK TO THE VEDAS"

OPPOSED to the "Science-Grounded Religion" among the many new forms of Hinduism, there is a "Vedic Religion," known as the Arya Samaj, the largest and most influential Hindu reform movement in India. As Muhammad is the key to Muhammadanism, and Buddha to Buddhism, so Swami Dayanand Sarasvati is the key to the Arya Samaj.

Mul Shankar was born in 1824 in the protected state of Morvi, Kathiawar, son of Amba Shankar, a Shaivite Brahman and well-to-do banker. Both Swami Dayanand and Mahatma Gandhi were born in that same western half of India, which from time immemorial has been ethnologically modified by repeated invasions. Like his father Mul Shankar had a strong will. As a Brahman, he never suffered from an inferiority complex. His education was in the vernacular, but as a lad he learned by heart large pieces of Sanskrit religious literature. He never learned English.

His biographers point out three moments of special interest in the home-life (1824-1845) of Mul Shankar. First, on his initiation at the age of fourteen in the temple of Shiva he saw mice running over the image of Shiva, and so lost all faith in the worship of idols. Second, at the age of eighteen the death of his sister and uncle affected him, just as a similar experience affected Buddha. Third, at the age of twenty-one he fled from home in order to escape from the entanglement of marriage. It is probable that his rejection of idolatry was caused by a larger group of circumstances than the mere experience in the temple of Shiva. The *Sthanakavasi* sect of non-idolatrous Jains was very influential in the neighborhood of Mul Shankar's birthplace, where there was doubtless a diffused atmosphere of thought and feeling, unfavorable to idolatry.[1] The early history of the life of Mul Shankar may be summarized thus: (1) in the negative determination to eschew idolatry; (2) in the positive determination to seek deliverance or *mukti;* and (3) in the further resolution to allow no such entanglement as marriage to interfere with this supreme purpose. Certain characteristics of the man are shadowed forth in these youthful experiences—his hatred of idolatry, his sensitiveness to new experiences, and his great firmness of will. His revolt from idolatry was complete, as is proved by the magnificent courage and vigor with which he afterwards attacked it in its chief centers, Benares and Hardwar.

The second stage of the life of Mul Shankar (1845-1863) is the period of his mendicant wanderings and

[1] See Farquhar, *Modern Religious Movements in India*, pp. 103-104.

religious studies. It was as it were a modern quest of the Holy Grail, the truth which should set India free, the "cup, of healing," which should heal India of her "grievous wound." He began with Vedantic teachers, and received initiation into the Sarasvati order of Shankara Dandis with the new name Dayananda Sarasvati. Soon, however, he surrendered the Vedanta standpoint, but he always remained an ascetic and to the end retained the new name. For the next eight years he pursued the study of Yoga, both classical and Tantric. Coming to question the Tantric anatomy of the human frame with its *nadis, Kundalini, Sushumna,* etc., he finally set his doubts at rest, as the story goes, by pulling a dead body from the river and dissecting it. His Tantric books went into the river. His final studies were conducted under the tuition of the blind Swami Virajananda of Mathura (1860-1863), an enemy of modern Sanskrit literature. With him he studied Panini's *Grammar* and the Vedanta-Sutras, and was dismissed with the charge to "Spread the Knowledge of the true Shastras, and *fight against the prevailing false sects.*" Thus his religious development was a movement from Pauranic Hinduism through Philosophical Hinduism to Vedic Hinduism. He surrendered successively Shaivism, Vedantism and Tantrism, but clung to the last to the *Sankhya-Yoga* as the philosophical point of view from which the Vedas ought to be interpreted. Already the founder of the Arya Samaj had revealed a capacity for change, a willingness to surrender previously formed opinions, an attitude which is embodied in the fourth principle of the Arya Decalogue, namely, that "one should always be ready to accept truth and renounce untruth."

The long apprenticeship of nearly forty years was followed by his public ministry (1863-1883). It was a period of preaching tours throughout India, of public discussions with pundits, maulvies, and missionaries, and of literary work, with now and then a retreat for further contemplation and perfection of character. In 1868 he met the missionary, the Reverend J. J. Scott. He clashed with the Benares pundits over the question, "Do the Vedas teach idolatry?" In 1872 he interviewed at Calcutta Keshab Chander Sen and Debendranath Tagore, and Ramakrishna as well. As a consequence of his meeting with the two Brahmo leaders, Swami Dayanand began to wear regular clothes and to use the vernacular Hindi rather than Sanskrit. At Allahabad in 1874 he completed his chief work, the *Satyartha Prakasha* (Light of truth). And in Bombay he came into touch with the Prarthana Samaj.

The Arya Samaj was founded by Swami Dayanand in Bombay, April 10, 1875. The main features of the new society were modelled after the Brahmo Samaj and Prarthana Samaj, but organic union with the two Samajes was prevented by Dayanand's conviction of the infallibility of the Vedas and the truth of transmigration. In 1877 Swami Dayanand visited the Punjab, the scene of the future triumphs of the

Samaj, and the headquarters were moved from Bombay to Lahore. A little later (1878-1881) there was the curious episode of a partnership between the Arya Samaj and the Theosophical Society, but soon that partnership was dissolved over the question of the personality of God.

Swami Dayanand died at Ajmer, October 30, 1883, under circumstances that gave rise to the suspicion that he had been poisoned, but of this there is no clear proof. He had played the part of a modern John the Baptist in rebuking the Maharaja of Jodhpur for being under the influence of a courtesan. A man of great strength of will, absolutely fearless, of magnificent presence, a leader of men–such was Swami Dayanand Sarasvati. He helped to stem the tide of pessimism, and to recover for India the Vedic optimism.

Swami Dayanand's problem was the regeneration of India–religious, social, political, and scientific. As he wandered over India, he found himself confronted by a variety of faiths both indigenous and foreign. Of religions of foreign origin he found Islam, which had been introduced in the tenth century, and Christianity (with the exception of the Syrian form), a comparatively recent importation from the West. The indigenous religion of India, Hinduism, presented itself as a vast congeries of faiths, ranging all the way from the strict *advaita* doctrine of Shankara to the crudest and grossest superstitions embodied in the Tantras, the whole being held together in a kind of external unity by the vast hierarchical organization of caste. This was the religious environment. As for the political environment, India was under foreign domination and everywhere the vast network of the British administration was in evidence. Railways, telegraph lines, and irrigation systems constituted a scientific environment. And all that came under his eye helped to set the problem for Swami Dayanand.

Now, as we have seen, Dayanand was a Hindu protestant. A Brahman monk, he became emancipated from Brahman orthodoxy in some such way as Luther, the German monk, became emancipated from Roman orthodoxy. Luther appealed from the Roman Church and the authority of tradition to the Scriptures of the Old and New Testament. Pundit Dayanand appealed from the Brahmanical Church and the authority of *smriti* (tradition) to the earliest and most sacred of Indian Scriptures. The watchword of Luther was "Back to the Bible" and the watchword of Dayanand was "Back to the Vedas." With this religious watchword another was implicitly, if not explicitly, combined, namely, "India for the Indians"—in other words, Indian *religion* for the Indians and Indian *sovereignty* for the Indians. To accomplish the first end Indian religion was to be reformed and purified by a return to the Vedas, and foreign religions such as Islam and Christianity were to be extirpated. The sections of the *Satyarth Prakash* which deal with the criticism of Islam and

Christianity are evidently intended to be the literature of such extirpation. To accomplish the second end, the founder of the Arya Samaj seems to have taught that a return to the pure teachings of the Vedas would gradually fit the people of India for self-rule, and that independence would ultimately be granted. Certainly most well-wishers of India hope that in some form or other *Swaraj* may soon come, indeed, may be already at the door. Because of the present *Swaraj* movement one may rightly reckon Swami Dayanand Sarasvati among the creators of modern India.

It is evident that Dayanand Sarasvati was a man of large views. He was a dreamer of splendid dreams. He had a vision of India purged of her superstitions, filled with the fruits of science, worshipping one God, fitted for self-rule, occupying a place in the sisterhood of nations, and restored to her ancient glory. All this was to be accomplished by throwing overboard the accumulated superstitions of the centuries and returning to the pure teachings of the Vedas. So the founder of the Arya Samaj may be thought of as a kind of Indian Elijah who felt himself called to turn the hearts of the degenerate children of modern India to their fathers of the glorious Vedic age, to reconcile the present with the past. The character of his mission helps to account for the violence of his methods of controversy. Elijah was not especially gentle in his dealings with the prophets of Baal; nor was Luther very tender toward the Roman Church.

In like manner Pundit Dayanand Sarasvati stood with his back to the wall, facing on the one hand the attacks of the Brahmanical hierarchy and on the other the assaults of the foreign religions, Islam and Christianity. Under these circumstances one can hardly wonder that he struck back as hard as he could. And surely his vision of a regenerated India is a splendid and inspiring one.

Dayanand took over from Brahmanical orthodoxy the theory of the Veda as God's eternal utterance [2] and the related view that the four Vedas were revealed to four sages, Agni, Vayu, Surya and Angiras, at the beginning of the present mundane age millions of years ago. It is a doctrine of "primitive revelation" with a vengeance. As eternal, the Vedas can contain no references to the local or temporal. All such apparent allusions are explained away: they are inconsistent with the eternity of the Vedas. It is the high *a priori* road in exegesis. Such a view of the immeasurable antiquity of the Vedas is a commentary on the historical and critical acumen of Swami Dayanand. No wonder that the late Lala Lajpat Rai found it impossible to go the whole length in such doctrines.

When Swami Dayanand compared the ancient lore of India, as set forth in the eternal Vedas, with the modern science of the West, as illustrated in railways, the telegraph, and like products of applied science, his problem was to effect a synthesis in such a way as

[2] *Manu,* I, 21-23; XII, 94-100.

to do full justice to the achievements of Western science and at the same time to guarantee the spiritual supremacy of the East. He found the key to the desired synthesis in a doctrine of double revelation, first, through the eternal Veda as revealed in the form of the four Vedas, and second, through the world of Nature. The Vedas constitute the pattern according to which creation proceeded. Hence the revelation of the Veda and the revelation in Nature correspond as the two halves of one whole. If then the scientific interpretation of nature is the achievement of the West, the scientific programme, as regards at least basic principles is the possession of the East, being found only in the four Vedas. In this way Swami Dayanand sought to render to the West the things that belong to the West, and to the East the things that belong to the East.

The Dayanandi doctrine of Vedic Scripture may be summarized as follows: First, the Vedas are a revelation from God, as is proved by their correspondence with nature; second, they are the sole revelation from God, since no other books show this correspondence; third, they are, accordingly, the fountain-head of the science and of the religion of mankind. Implicit in this doctrine is the view that all the religions of the world, including Islam and Christianity, are simply garbled and degenerate forms of the primitive Vedic revelation. Hence all religions are bound sooner or later to succumb before the triumphant march of the eternal Vedic religion. Such is the philosophy of religion as held by the Arya Samaj. On this doctrinal basis rest the two great religious duties of the Samaj: to recall India to the forsaken Vedic paths, and to preach the Vedic gospel throughout the whole world.

The Dayanandi interpretation of the Vedas may be characterized as highly subjective and fanciful, different meanings being applied to the same word according to the caprice of the interpreter. Thus there is great emphasis on etymology and neglect of actual Vedic usage, together with the assumption of irregularity in the Vedic moods, tenses, persons, and cases. By such a method the Vedas are made to contain the germs of absolutely all knowledge, including the knowledge of scientific inventions such as the steam engine, electric telegraph, etc. As Max Müller puts it: "By the most incredible interpretations Swami Dayanand succeeded in persuading himself and others that everything worth knowing, even the most recent inventions of modern science, were alluded to in the Vedas."[3] *A priorism* reigns supreme. Induction has no place. Hence the doctrines of the Arya Samaj, especially as regards the scientific discoveries of modern times, are based, not on the Vedas themselves, but on an uncritical and unscientific interpretation thereof. The honesty of Swami Dayanand in explaining the Vedas in this way has been impugned by Pundit S. N. Agnihotri.[4] But other incredible

[3] *Biographical Essays,* II, 170.
[4] *Pandit Dayanand Unveiled,* 1891.

methods of interpretation are found in the history of exegesis. Undoubtedly the results aimed at have not infrequently a way of influencing the methods employed, without any conscious dishonesty on the part of the writers.

The central point in the theology of Swami Dayanand is his doctrine of God. What are the steps by which he moved from the Shaiva doctrine of his early home onward to the monotheism of his mature life and teaching? We cannot be sure, but we can hazard some reasonable conjectures. A kind of monotheism, albeit of an unstable character, is implicit in Hinduism.[5] The Shaivism of Dayanand's early days represents such a monotheism, since the worshipper of Shiva in certain moods regards him as identical with the *Brahma* of the Upanishads. There was at least a bent toward monotheism in Shaivism, and it was not difficult for Swami Dayanand, even from the point of view of popular Hinduism, to recognize Shiva (in 1866) as only one of the many names of god. Moreover, Swami Dayanand's doctrine of God may have been influenced by the indigenous development of Hindu theism in several stages, the Varuna hymns of the Rigveda, the Yoga or "theistic Sankhya," the theism of Ramanuja, and the theism of the Brahmo Samaj. The Sankhya-Yoga probably furnished the Arya trinity—God, matter, and soul. The theism of Ramanuja and of the

[5] See Art. *Brahmanism and Hinduism* by H. D. Griswold, in *Encyclopædia of the Social Sciences*, 1930, Vol. II, p. 676.

Brahmo Samaj undoubtedly provided the doctrine of the real and eternal personality of God.

But the founder of the Arya Samaj may have been influenced by still other considerations, derived from the foreign religions, Islam and Christianity. He must have noticed that each of these religions had a compact and definite creed, that they were both growing relatively faster than Hinduism, and that it was obviously only a question of time for them to win the day, unless the adverse tide were checked. He must have seen clearly that to check the growth of Islam and Christianity an indigenous monotheism having their virility and militant character must be discovered or created. He doubtless felt that it must be a distinctly Indian monotheism, not like that of the Brahmo Samaj with its international platform and all-embracing creed. The many gods of the Rigveda, accordingly, he interpreted as diverse names for the one God. This was not especially difficult, since the Vedic nature gods may well have been conceived as visible representations of a single invisible Reality; and besides priests and poets are declared to have changed by words the One into the many in certain late passages which seem to indicate that the One represents reality while the many are more or less artificial and illusory.

Whatever the causes, the effect was a brief creed in the form of Ten Principles—three theological and seven ethical. The first principle sets forth the doctrine of *One God alone to be worshipped spiritually, not by images.* The whole creed, so colorless and general that almost any theist might subscribe to it, looks as if it were intended primarily for the purpose of foreign propaganda. The real working creed consists of the Fifty-one Teachings of Dayanand.[6] Thus was produced an Indian theism, designed to rival the foreign theisms, Christianity and Islam. It left almost everything intact in Hinduism except polytheism and idolatry. These things were not found in the foreign theisms, nor in the Vedas as interpreted by Swami Dayanand, hence must not be found in the new-born Indian theism. In doctrine and polity Swami Dayanand kept so close to orthodox Hinduism that there was no violent break involved in passing from the Sanatana Dharma to the Arya Samaj. This all represents an extremely clever move on his part. It was a noteworthy achievement to found an indigenous theism, non-polytheistic and non-idolatrous, right in the very home of pantheism, polytheism, and idolatry! He has drawn a large number of educated Hindus into his society, has won them to the worship of one God, and has instilled into them a strenuous and optimistic spirit. In these respects, the Dayanandi theism is akin to Christianity and Islam, and is to be reckoned among the important theisms of the world.

The theology of Swami Dayanand is undergirded by the philosophy of the Sankhya-Yoga, the Sankhya

[6] See for the "Ten Principles" and the Fifty-one Teachings of Dayanand, Lajpat Rai, *Arya Samaj,* p. 81 ff. and 101 ff.

contributing matter (*prakriti*) and soul (*purusha*) and the Yoga contributing God. But, not to mention the fact that the god of the Yoga was an afterthought introduced as a concession to popular prejudice, the doctrine of three separate, self-existent, and eternal entities, namely, God, soul, and matter, is open to grave objection. If God is eternally confronted by souls and matter for which He is in no way responsible, not having created them, then there is no unifying principle in the universe. The soul is declared to be a *free* agent, because it is eternally separate from God and matter and so not conditioned by either. Salvation is through continued well-doing. Transmigration and Karma, though not found in the hymns of the Rigveda, belong to the Dayanandi soteriology. Salvation is conceived as virtually an eternal process of gaining, on the basis of good works, higher and higher births. There is no such thing as remission of sin. Karma is inexorable.

One wonders why in Swami Dayanand's system of social reform, which in general is ethically progressive, there is included *Niyoga,* or temporary marriage. It is well known that levirate marriage (that is, marriage of a widow with her deceased husband's brother) was sanctioned in Hinduism as in Hebraism. Swami Dayanand extended the theory of Niyoga, as laid down in the Hindu scriptures, vastly beyond the original permission. He observed that both Islam and Christianity permit widows to marry again and that such remarriage increases population.

So, without interfering with the Hindu prejudice against the remarriage of widows, he offered a plan to meet the loss of population thereby entailed—the doctrine of *Niyoga,* by which widows could be utilized apart from marriage for the procreation of offspring. This is the most questionable point in the ethics of Swami Dayanand.

From orthodox Hinduism he borrowed the doctrine of the eternity and the infallibility of the Vedas. This was all the easier for the reason that to the ordinary Hindu the Vedas are, like Tibet, an unknown region, about which no assertion can be accurately checked. He also took over the doctrines of transmigration and Karma, and the conception of salvation as release from transmigration. Some other orthodox doctrines he rejected, as, for example, the authority of the Brahman who is a Brahman only by birth; the restriction of Vedic study to the "twice-born"; polytheism, pantheism, and idolatry; the theory of divine incarnations; the conception of the soul's release as absorption into, or identity with, Brahma. And he rejected the late Pauranic writings.

What then, are the things that are significant in the Dayanandi theological and ethical system? Negatively, the revolt from popular Hinduism, the rejection of pantheism and of some of the doctrines included therein, such as illusion and absorption, the casting over of the Pauranic superstitions together with idolatry, and a more or less vigorous fight against certain hurtful social customs, such as caste, child-marriage, and intemperance. Positively, the promulgation of a fairly consistent theism, the doctrine of the personality of God, and of the eternal identity of the soul, belief in prayer and in the value of the social worship of God, and a certain enthusiasm for moral reform especially along the lines of education and of domestic and social life.

The Arya Samaj is a social and political quite as much as a religious name. It means literally "the society of the Aryans," not the society of God, as the Brahmo Samaj and early Deva Samaj mean. The officers—president, vice-president, secretary, treasurer, and librarian—are such as commonly represent a secular association. In 1892 the Samaj suffered a schism into two sections, the College or "Cultured" section with its educational center at Lahore, and the Vegetarian or "Mahatma" section with its educational center at Hardwar. The cultured party are the modernists of the Arya Samaj, and stand for up-to-date educational methods, for freedom in diet, and also for freedom in the matter of accepting the interpretations of Swami Dayanand. The first man who transgressed the limits of permitted freedom was the late Lajpat Rai, who was practically excommunicated. The Mahatma party, on the other hand, as the fundamentalists of the Arya Samaj, stand for the *Gurukul* system of ancient Hindu education, for a vegetarian diet, and for a strict acceptance of the teachings of Dayanand.

The conditions of membership are acceptance of

the canons of Vedic interpretation laid down by Swami Dayanand and implicit faith in the Arya "Decalogue." Initiation involves for the "twice-born" classes nothing except the signing of the Decalogue, but for Muhammadans, Christians, and all Hindus except the "twice-born" a ceremony of purification is necessary. Several grades of members are recognized, approved or voting members, probationers or non-voting members, and perhaps a third class of sympathizers. There are local samajes, provincial assemblies, and a General Assembly for all India.

The Arya meetings for worship are held on Sunday, the public offices being closed on that day. A service is three or four hours long, but people may come and go whenever they like. The first part of the service, usually sparsely attended, consists of the ritual of the Vedic fire altar, the burning of incense, and the chanting of Vedic hymns. The second part —prayers, hymns, sermon, etc.—is like an ordinary Protestant Christian service, and is puritan in its simplicity. There is no official priesthood. The Arya Samaj represents a stern reaction against the priesthood of orthodox Hinduism.

The methods of work are the ordinary missionary methods, such as preaching, education, literature, newspapers, orphanages, work among the depressed classes. Preachers are of two types, paid and honorary. Among the societies that may be mentioned are the Arya Tract Society, Women's Arya Samaj, Young Men's Arya Association, and Vedic Salvation Army. All of these names suggest the imitation of Christian methods of propaganda. The Arya Samaj has sought to outflank the Christian missionary movement. From one point of view it may be regarded as a defense mechanism to meet the impact of Christianity and Islam.

Notable educational institutions are the Dayanand Anglo-Vedic College, Lahore, founded in 1886 as a memorial of Swami Dayanand. In point of numbers it is the largest College in the Punjab. The first Principal, Lala Hans Raj, served without salary, and several graduates of the College have received as professors only a subsistence allowance. The *Gurukula Mahavidyalaya* at Hardwar was founded in 1902, has a seventeen-year course for boys from the age of eight to twenty-five, and practices a Spartan discipline, parents being allowed to interview their sons for only fifteen minutes each year. There is an important boarding school for girls at Jullunder, and the Raja Ram College at Kolhapur.

Lala Lajpat Rai admits the imitation of Christian methods of philanthropic work. "Outside Christian circles it [the Arya Samaj] was the first purely Indian association to organize Orphanages and Widow Homes." "The Arya Samaj was the first non-Christian private agency which started a non-official movement for the relief of distress caused by famine." "There is now a network of social service agencies throughout India, due mainly to the contact of the

East with the West, and to the example of Christian Missionary enterprise." [7]

The growth of membership in the Arya Samaj has been phenomenal. The Government Census reports for 1891, 1901, 1911, and 1921 give, respectively, 39,952, 92,419, 245,000 (*circa*) and 467,578. Of the 467,578 Aryas for 1921, the Punjab, Delhi and Kashmir had 246,000, the United Provinces 205,000, and all the rest of India only some 16,000. The Arya Samaj, therefore, is a Punjab and United Provinces movement, and has had its greatest success in those provinces where the invading Aryan stock is more largely represented. The name *Arya* Samaj was happily chosen for it accepts as its supremely authoritative Scripture only the four Vedas, and especially the Rigveda, which is the purest expression of the Aryan spirit on the soil of India.

As stated in the opening sentence, Swami Dayanand is the key to the Arya Samaj. His leading characteristics are reproduced in the society he founded. He bequeathed to it a forceful and optimistic spirit, an attitude and temper Aryan and Vedic. Dayanand and his Samaj have done much toward naturalizing in modern India the old Vedic optimism. No inferiority complex characterized Dayanand and his followers any more than it characterized the early Vedic Aryans. Swami Dayanand was also non-mystical and rationalistic, therein differing widely from most Hindu religious personalities. He banished from his

[7] Lajpat Rai, *Arya Samaj*, pp. 211-212, 219.

system the mystical notion of the illusory nature of sense experience as well as that of the absorption of the finite soul into, or its identity with, the Supreme Soul. A mystical system like the Vedanta was rejected by him in favor of the realistic Sankhya-Yoga. The burning of incense in worship is given no special mystical significance: it is enough to say that "it purifies the air." In his method of Vedic interpretation he followed the high *a priori* road of deduction as the great method of proof. As the founder of the largest indigenous reform movement in India Swami Dayanand Sarasvati may well be called a Builder of Modern India.

CHAPTER XI

THE RADHA SOAMI SATSANG, A SEMI-SECRET RELIGIOUS SOCIETY

LIKE a temple which is open to the people, except for the Holy of Holies, where only priests may enter, so the Radha Soami Society has an exoteric side open to outsiders and an esoteric side confined to members alone.[1] My chief authority for the more hidden doctrines and practices of the sect was a man who had left the society after having been a member for about thirteen years.

The founder and first *guru* was Tulsi Ram, better known as Shiv Dayal Sahib (1818-1878), an Agra banker of the Kshatriya order and Vaishnavite religion. The very title of the sect, Radha Soami, indicates its Vaishnavite affinity. Tulsi Ram had a *guru,* Tulsi Sahib, who doubtless gave a special bent to his disciple's thinking. Tulsi Ram began to proclaim his doctrine in 1861, and as the *Sant Satguru* (holy preceptor) gathered disciples. He taught a system of secret meditation and practice (*yoga*), which induced trances and other hypnotic results. Like Swami

1 In the matter of secrecy one may compare the Deva Samaj, the Shamsis, whose head is the Aga Khan, and the Jaikishnias, who are the same as the Manbhaus of Western India.

Dayanand and Ramakrishna Paramahansa, Tulsi Ram had no Western education. He left, however, two books, *Sar Bachan* (Essential Utterance), one in poetry and one in prose. On his tomb in the Radha Soami Garden, Agra, there is a picture of the first *guru* and his wife as *Krishna* and *Radha,* which may furnish the key to the name of the sect.

The second *guru,* Saligram Sahib (1828-1898), was born in Agra of the Kayasth, or writer caste. He rose to the position of Postmaster General of the United Provinces and received from Government the title of *Rai Bahadur.* As head of the sect (1878-1898), he perfected its organization, gave it its name, and formulated its theology. His works are in Hindi.[2]

Third in the *guru* succession came Brahma Shankar Mishra, a Bengali Brahman (1898-1907). He, like Swami Vivekananda, was an M.A. of the Calcutta University. He held a position in the Accountant General's office, Allahabad. With the exception of a few poems in Hindi his works are in English.[3] After the death of the third *guru* there was the danger of a schism into two sections.[4]

The real meaning of *Radhasvami*[5] is Lord of

[2] Their titles, as translated, are: *Love Utterances, Love Letters,* and *Exposition of Radha Soami Doctrine.*

[3] Two brief expositions for the Census of 1901, *Discourses on Radha Soami Faith,* and *Solace to Satsangis, or members of the society.*

[4] The Protestant sects of Hinduism, e.g., Brahmo Samaj, Arya Samaj, Deva Samaj, etc., show the same tendency to division as is shown by the Protestant sects of Christianity.

[5] Spelled by the sect, *Radha Soami.*

Radha, that is Krishna. According to Farquhar, on the basis of the photograph of the first *guru* and his wife on their tombs in Agra, the two names Radha and Swami were probably applied to them, and then to God as perfectly represented by the *guru*.[6] At any rate, Radha Soami is used first, as the name of God himself; second, as the Word, or emanation from God in the form of a spiritual sound-current; third, as the name the first *guru* bears as the perfect incarnation of God; and, fourth, as the name of the sect conceived as pervaded by the energy or spirit of God.[7]

The key to the theology of the Radha Soami community is to be found in its cosmology. The universe has three grand divisions: *material-spiritual* region, where matter is primary and spirit secondary, the region of individual mind, with six sub-divisions; *spiritual-material* region, where spirit is primary and matter secondary, "the region of universal mind," with five sub-divisions; and the region of *pure spirit,* spirit uncontaminated with matter, called "the region of mercy," with seven sub-divisions. All this indicates that the sect holds a realistic doctrine of matter as something different from mind, although it may exist in combination with mind. In harmony with this we are told that the Radhasoamis "recog-

[6] *Modern Religious Movements,* p. 167 and E.R.E., X, 559.

[7] One may compare the group of meanings carried by *brahman* in the early literature, namely sacred word, mysterious potency, Ultimate Reality (God), and the Brahman order as pervaded by *brahman.* See *Brahman: a Study of Indian Philosophy,* 1900, by H. D. Griswold, pp. iv, 20.

nize the separate existence of God, the soul, and matter," and are opposed to the doctrine of *advaita.*[8] This is good Ramanuja doctrine and is a point of contact with the Arya Samaj. The three grand divisions are dominated, respectively, by the notions of body, of mind, and of spirit, suggesting a parallelism between the individual and the universe, man a microcosm standing over against the macrocosm. The third *guru* declares that "the human frame represents on a small scale the whole creation." [9] This being so, the eighteen sub-divisions of the macrocosmos are to be found in miniature in the microcosmos. The six sub-divisions of the lowest region, microcosmically considered, are the six nervous centers or ganglia found in the spinal cord, connected in an ascending order with the rectum, reproductive organ, navel, heart, throat, and the point between the two eyes, known as the pineal gland. The centers of the second grand division are in the gray matter of the brain, and those of the purely spiritual region in the white matter. The eighteen stages are as it were milestones on the way of the soul's spiritual progress from the *Ganesh Chakkar* at the bottom, with its seat in the rectum, upward to the Radha Soami Dham at the top, the realm of "light infinite and incomparable." Salvation consists in successfully completing this pilgrimage.

[8] *Census of India,* 1901, Vol. XVI, p. 79.

[9] Compare *The Hindu Conception of the Functions of Breath,* Part II, p. 44, by A. H. Ewing, J. A. O. S., 1902.

The Supreme Being, *Radha Soami,* as Lord of the highest stage and pure spirit, is unknown,[10] but can be known indirectly through the appearance periodically in human form of "Beloved Sons" in order to deliver men from the bondage of matter. The *Radha Soami Gurus* are such beloved sons.

Next in importance to the doctrine of God is the doctrine of the Word (*Shabda*), which has been given the name *Radha Soami* by the Supreme Being Himself in His incarnation as the first *guru.* It is an emanation from the Supreme Being in the form of a "Spirit or Sound-current," which streams through all regions, sounding forth the divine name *Radha Soami.* This is the supreme agent in creation.[11]

Soami, the Great First Cause, as "the mysterious source of all energy," is the *"Supreme Father"* (*paramapita*). *Radha,* the "spirit-current," emanating, in the form of energy, from *Soami,* and going forth on a creative errand, is the "Supreme Mother" (*Paramamata*). *Radha* reveals *Soami,* for *Radha* is to *Soami* as the rays of the sun to the sun. In Gnostic phraseology *Soami* is the "original æon" and *Radha* the "first emanation" from the bosom of the abyss. The two names combined furnish the title of the "Supreme Being." The *Sant Satguru,* as an incarnation of the invisible God, is the "Supreme Son." There

10 Compare the Upanishadic *"Neti, Neti,"* and the Gnostic view of God as the "unfathomable abyss."

11 Compare the creative Logos in John I, 1-3 and Kabir's doctrine of *Shabd,* the Creative Word.

is a succession of Supreme Sons, unless we are to regard the founder Shiv Dayal Sahib as the "Supreme Son" *par excellence,* and his successors as in a lesser sense "supreme sons." So the Radha Soami theology has a trinity, which resembles slightly the Christian doctrine.

The Supreme Being, *Radha Soami,* is conceived differently in the three grand divisions of the cosmological scheme. In the highest division, the realm of pure spirit, He (or it) is *impersonal* and unknown, and is likened to an Ocean. Here He reigns over absolutely spiritual life.[12]

Radha Soami is *personal* in the second division, or region of universal mind and pure matter. As the Viceroy, who presides over this, He is a tide from the Ocean of the Supreme, and is identified with the Lord God of the Bible, the Brahman (neut.) of the Vedanta, the Nirvana of the Jains and Buddhists, and the Lahut of the Muslim [13] saints.

Radha Soami is *personal* in the third division, the sphere of gross matter and individual mind. The Governor of this is likened to a wave from the tide which emanates from the Ocean of the Supreme. He

[12] The two highest stages are peopled by the successive heads of the Radha Soami sect, the next two by Kabir and Tulsi Sahib, *guru* of Shiv Dayal Sahib, and the twelfth stage by Guru Nanak, Dadu Sahib, Sur Das, Charan Das, *et. al.*, and also by the Muslim mystics, Maulana Rum and Bu Ali Sahib Kalandar.

[13] The second cosmological division is peopled by various incarnations, Rama and Krishna, the Rishis and Munis, Jesus Christ (seventh stage), and Muhammad (sixth stage, reckoning from the bottom).

is the Brahma (masc.) of the Hindus, and the god of most religions.[14]

Man is conceived as originally a pure drop from the Ocean of the Supreme Being, but as now entangled with matter and so in bondage, and in danger of sinking lower and lower.[15] Having forgotten the place from which they originally came, namely the Ocean of God, the spirits of the world of matter have acquired carnal desires.

The source of deliverance is the Supreme Being, *Radha Soami,* who manifests himself to humanity in the person of the *Sant Satguru,* who is the only way to God. We come now to the secret-discipline, called *Surat-Shabda-Yoga,* literally Spirit-Word-Yoga, that is the "union of the human spirit with the Word." The sound-current which emanates from the Supreme goes forth in creation and returns, as it were redemptively, to its original source, God. The current, which, through its creative work has brought the human spirit down here, must naturally be the only true path for its return to the original source. Whoever connects himself with this current is on the way to emancipation.

[14] We may note here the apparent recognition of Shankara's distinction between "lower knowledge" and "higher knowledge," since in the third and second divisions the Supreme Being, *Radha Soami,* is under the illusion of sense seen only as He appears to be, in distorted and demonic forms, whereas in the highest division He is seen as He really is.

[15] Note the doctrine of a fall of man and the conception of matter as evil. Compare the Sankhya doctrine of evil as the result of the union of *purusha* (man), with *prakriti* (matter), and the Vedanta doctrine of the *atman* (spirit), as wrapped up in *maya* so that it cannot recognize its true nature.

What, then, is the method of riding the life, or sound current, so as to make the journey home to God? It consists in a concentration at the focus of the eyes, of the attention, which is usually diffused and tied to external objects. First, the novice with eyes closed is to fixate in thought the point between the eyes and see in imagination either his *guru* or the flame of a lamp, meanwhile saying over and over, "*Radha Soami.*" [16] Next the novice places both hands upon his forehead, the two little fingers coming togther at the point between the eyes, and the two thumbs pressing the two ears shut; and in this attitude, he seeks to reproduce the experiences of the first lesson and in addition to recognize the sound of a bell. In this way, the novice learns successively the special characteristics of each of the eighteen spheres of existence, namely, presiding deity, peculiar light, musical sound, and special name, and by the prescribed yoga practice seeks to enter into an experimental realization especially of the musical sounds. For, to obtain spiritual benefit, the sounds issuing from the highest division must be heard internally.

The work of emancipation is helped or hindered by one's manner of life. All acts which tend to raise the spirit higher towards its source are good, and all that tend to depress it lower and lower are bad. Ascordingly, animal food, the use of intoxicating drinks and drugs, and all immoderation in things allowable

[16] It looks like a process of self-hypnotism.

are forbidden; and such practices as attending fairs, engaging in political agitation, the wearing of gorgeous apparel, excessive sleep, and idle conversation are discouraged. In fact, the Radha Soami movement represents a type of Hindu Puritanism.

Closely connected with *Surat-Shabda-Yoga,* and a necessary part of it, is *guru*-worship. Worship of the "Supreme Father," who is in himself unknowable, is largely through the worship of his incarnation, the "Supreme Son." Such *guru*-worship[17] consists of prostration before the Supreme Son or his photograph, belief that everything that has touched his body is filled with spiritual potency, eating certain products of his body, drinking the water with which he has bathed his feet, and after his death swallowing his ashes mixed with water.

A public religious meeting of the Radha Soami is very simple, consisting of singing, reading from the sacred scriptures of the sect, and an address. The canon of holy scripture consists of the writings of the successive *Sant Sat-gurus,* and next in importance the writings of Kabir and Nanak and certain other Hindu saints.

The Radha Soami Satsang has had a steady growth. A membership of about 100,000 is claimed for 1928, found largely in the Punjab, United Provinces, and Bengal. Their program, like that of every reforming movement in modern India, is universalistic. People

[17] See *Radha Swami Sect* by H. D. Griswold, pp. 14-15, and compare the methods of *Guru*-worship in the Deva Samaj.

of all castes and nationalities and religions are received, and it is expected that the whole world will finally embrace the Radha Soami faith. "It is quite optional to believers to renounce publicly their former creed or not."[18] It is their theory that all religions are in a sense true, and that the Radha Soami faith is fitted to be the complement of any and every religion, and *supreme* over them all. Outside the Radha Soami church, they believe, there is no salvation, that is, no possibility of emancipation from rebirth. It is admitted, however, that all religions may give some help in the initial stages of the soul's spiritual progress.

Theoretically, caste is not observed, but the prejudices of weak brethren are respected.

The chief method of propaganda is the witness-bearing of individual members to the high qualities of the "Revered Leader."[19] So far as known, there is no foreign propaganda.

The points that attract new members are the following: a secret religious society; the mystery of the *Surat-Shabda-Yoga* with its promise of power and beatific vision; the living *guru* an incarnation of God; no break with one's old religion; freedom of different castes within the meetings of the sect; the claim that "the religion is based on purely scientific

[18] *Census of India,* 1901, Vol. XVI, p. 80. Compare the practice of Theosophy.

[19] A student of mine in the Forman Christian College, Lahore, once spoke to me in the highest terms of his Radha Soami *guru*.

grounds"; and the reputation of the Radha Soami *gurus* for spiritual insight and holiness of life.

The sect has certain affinities with Vaishnavism, as indicated by the name *Radha Svami,* a realistic conception of God, the soul and matter, the notion that the soul is a portion of God, the *Shakti* or energy of God in the form of a "spirit-current," and transmigration. It resembles Gnosticism in holding that matter is essentially evil, that creation is the result of spirit somehow falling under the power of matter, and that salvation consists in the deliverance of the spirit from the bondage of matter. It has numerous points of contact with Theosophy, such as the unknowable Supreme, the spheres and their regents, the human revealers of religion, esoteric teaching, methodical exercises, etc. It claims a close affinity with Science, there being much talk about waves, forces, currents, gray matter, white matter, pineal gland, etc. With Kabir the relationship is especially close in the doctrine of the Word, and an attempt is made, after the manner of comparative religion, to grade the religious leaders of the world according to their merit.

There are numerous affinities also with Christianity, such as the doctrine of a Supreme Father and a Supreme Son, a kind of trinity with a Supreme Mother (in place of the Christian Holy Spirit); incarnation; emphasis on love and works of faith and service; prayer; a supreme moral law; and a universal message for all mankind.

The religious and administrative center of the Radha Soami community since 1915 is at *Dayalbagh*, "the Garden of the Merciful," near the tomb of the founder outside of Agra. It consists of five hundred acres of land and has a resident Radha Soami population of about two thousand souls. It is the headquarters of the present (1928) head of the sect, His Holiness Sahabji Maharaj Anand Sarup Sahib. It is the educational center of the movement, having schools with industrial and academic departments for both boys and girls, co-education up to a certain point, and morning and evening worship. It has removed the earlier reproach that economic, literary, and educational progress form no part of the ideal of the sect, and has won hearty commendation and support from the educational officers of the Government. The sect has among its members many well-educated people, and in general has a high standard of literacy.

CHAPTER XII

JAINISM AND ITS CONTRASTS OF ASCETIC RENUNCIATION AND LAY PROSPERITY

IN THE sixth century B.C., several radical movements flourished in North India which issued in Jainism, Buddhism, and the Sankhya Philosophy. These in their origin represented a kind of protestant reaction on the part of the Kshatriyas against Brahman exclusiveness. The final outcome of Upanishad speculation had been the conception of an infinite number of finite spirits as a manifestation of the One Infinite and Supreme Spirit. The three protesting schools of thought accepted the doctrine of the multiplicity of finite spirits, or, as Buddha held, of finite consciousnesses, but rejected the doctrine of their reduction to one Infinite Spirit, God. In this sense each of the three systems mentioned above is "without God."

Jainism retains the Vedic animism. It is not, however, the speculative doctrine of the *atma* (spirit), but the empirical consciousness of the soul as "life" (*jiva*), which seems to have furnished the starting point for Jain animism.[1]

This animism appears in a highly exaggerated

[1] See Jacobi, S. B. E., XXII, 3, as quoted by Mrs. Stevenson, *The Heart of Jainism*, p. 95.

form, the Jains believing that there are "souls in every particle of earth, air, water and fire, as well as in men, animals and plants." [2] The problem of the ethical life of the Jain monk is to avoid injuring any one of these souls, for *ahinsa* (non-injury) is the supreme moral law of Jainism. One cannot help breathing air, but to hurt it as little as possible [3] the monks often wear a mouth-cloth. To avoid crushing insects, as one walks, they carry a brush with which to sweep the path. It is the doctrine of extreme *ahinsa;* and herein lies the paradoxical fact that the Kshatriya order, the proper business of which is fighting and killing, has given rise to a religion which is against the killing of any living thing.

Jainism retains the Upanishad doctrines of karma, transmigration, and release, interpreted according to the Sankhya philosophy. The supreme aim is *mukti* (release), the freeing of the soul from matter, and the endurance of austerities is a great help toward this end, for the sum of one's *karma* can be reduced by the fire of tapas. Fasting, depilation at regular intervals, and occasionally religious suicide by starvation are practiced. Jainism represents one of the most ancient monastic organizations of India, and its practice of asceticism is extreme. In most religions, for example, in Christianity, the ideal is the development of personality, but some aspects of Jainism sug-

[2] Farquhar, *Outline of the Religious Literature of India,* 1919, p. 74.

[3] Mrs. Stevenson, *The Heart of Jainism,* 1915, p. 100.

gest the negation of personality as the goal, the Jain ascetic beginning here and now the eliminating process.

Jainism in its origin was an older contemporary of Buddhism. Its founder, or at least first great teacher, was the Kshatriya, Vardhamana,[4] later called *Mahavira* (great hero), and *Jina* (conqueror). These are good Kshatriya titles and suggest heroism and victory as approved Jain qualities. Vardhamana at the age of thirty became a monk and for twelve years practised self-mortification, most of the time discarding even clothes. The first great schism (A.D. 83) was over the question, clothes or no clothes. It was a matter of climate as well as of the practice of the founder. The *Digambaras* (sky-clad), found mostly far south in Tamil land, maintained that sanctity requires nudity. Their idols are also nude, as in the rock sculptures around the Gwalior Fort. Since women cannot go naked, the Digambaras hold that they cannot win release until they are born as men.

The *Svetambaras* (white-clad) are the rival sect produced by the great schism. As the name indicates, all are clothed, images, ascetics and lay people alike. They are mainly found north of the Vindhya range. With them women as women may obtain release.

The two main divisions of Jainism hold almost identical doctrines, but refuse to intermarry or eat together. Naturally then they must have separate

[4] Born probably 599 B.C. not far from Patna in Eastern India. Buddha was born about 560 B.C.

temples. They have somewhat different canons of holy scripture, but agree in the worship paid to the twenty-four Tirthankaras, of whom Parshvanath and Mahavira, the last two, are probably alone historical. The worship of "perfected" men is a startling anticipation of positivism, the Jain pantheon consisting of a body of deified saints.[5]

The *Sthanakavasis* are one of the eighty-four schools into which the Svetambaras are divided. Non-idolatrous, they are the result of the second great schism over the question, idols or no idols. It was as a Jain puritan movement that the Sthanakavasi sect arose in 1653, contemporaneous with similar movements in Europe. Probably one can detect Moslem influence, for it was in A.D. 1452, at Ahmadabad, a city full of Muhammadans at that time, that the *Lonka*[6] disapproval of idolatry arose, a movement which prepared the way for the Sthanakavasis. We can probably trace the effect of the Sthanakavasi environment upon the youthful Mul Shankar (*alias* Swami Dayanand Sarasvati), leading him to give up idolatry once for all. And Mr. Gandhi, who was also born in a Sthanakavasi region, gives idolatry only a kind of negative support, saying, "I do not disbelieve in idolatry."

The Sthanakavasis are themselves divided into at least eleven sub-sects, one of which is the Terapanthi

[5] One may compare the Yoga, or Theistic Sankhya, in which some one soul, that has, on strict Sankhya premises, only attained release, is given apotheosis as God.

[6] Mrs. Stevenson, *op. cit.*, pp. 19, 87-88.

sect. The meaning of *Terapanthi* (whose path is *tera*) is uncertain. Some say it is so called because there were thirteen (*terah*) *sadhus*, when the sect was founded; others, that it is the sect that follows thirteen rules of conduct; and still others, that it is the sect of the Lord (*Tera* meaning "thine"). It was founded by Bhikanji, who in 1760 left the Sthankavasis. The present head of the Terapanthis is Swami Khaluramji, whom I once met at an annual function of the Terapanthi sect held in the Bikanir state.[7] The place was a village in a wild and semi-desert region. We were entertained in the rest-house of the Maharaja of Bikanir. As we entered the village, signs of wealth appeared on every hand, especially in the size and excellence of the houses. We found several hundred people gathered under a shamiana, a cloth covering stretched so as to keep off the sun, the head of the sect being enthroned in front, before him on the left about a hundred *Sadhus* and on his right over two hundred *Sadvis*, or women ascetics, and behind them the lay people, women on one side, men on the other. The contrast between the monks and nuns and the lay people was striking. The wives and daughters of the wealthy Marwari merchants were there in all their glory, dressed in purple and scarlet and fine linen, resplendent with costly jewels.

We stayed there for two or three days and had

[7] The occasion was the invitation extended by certain Marwari merchants of Calcutta to Dr. Charles Gilkey of Chicago, to meet the head of their sect.

opportunities for talking with both ascetics and laymen. Sanskrit was fairly well understood by the head of the sect and by some of the *sadhus*. A few of them had cloth tied over their mouths, and we heard a good deal about depilation, the custom in accordance with which each monk twice a year pulls the hair out of his own head by the roots. No images were seen, the sect being an offshoot of the Sthanakavasis and so non-idolatrous. We asked how they justified the destruction of life in seeds, which must be used for food. The answer received was not satisfactory. A modern Jain scholar, however, has frankly faced the difficulty, and his solution is that life is never to be destroyed, "unless it is necessary for the maintenance of a higher kind of life." [8] The Terapanthi lay folk number about 200,000, we were told, the ascetics, male and female, about 350. Great Marwari merchants had come all the way from Calcutta to be present at the meeting and to honor their *Guru*. We were impressed with the importance of the lay representation. In fact, one reason assigned by some scholars to account for the fact that, while Buddhism has perished from India, Jainism has survived, is the larger place given in Jainism to lay people. If, however, Buddhism has been banished from India, the land of its birth, Jainism has retreated from Magadha, the province in eastern India of its birth, and has found an asylum in southern and western India.

[8] Jagmanderlal Jaini, M.A., *Outlines of Jainism*, 1916, p. 71.

On another occasion some ten or fifteen years ago I found myself encamped with Dr. and Mrs. Bandy near the village of Kampil in the Farrukhabad district of North India. I did not know until afterward that Kampil was the ancient *Kampilya,* one of the capitals of the Kuru-Panchalas, a confederacy of Vedic tribes. We set out to explore two large buildings in the place. Both proved to be Jain temples, one for the "white-clad" and the other for the "sky-clad." Having removed our shoes, we were permitted to go anywhere we pleased. There were no Jains living in Kampil, and we wondered at the existence of Jain temples there. Afterwards it was learned that Kampilya was the traditional birthplace of Vimalanath, one of the twenty-four Jain Tirthankaras, great saints of the past who had attained perfection and release. The two temples were full of images of those who had received Jain beatification and so had become the objects of Jain worship. The officiant of the Digambara temple was a non-Jain Brahman, and of the other temple a Jain layman. In the course of my exploration I had reached the *adytum,* or holy of holies, of one of the temples, and was admiring the finely carved marble work, when suddenly in trooped a group of six or eight Jain pilgrims from near Bombay, both men and women. They proceeded to chant together a kind of litany and to make an offering of rice. I continued to stand immediately behind them. No priest was present. They officiated as their own priests. This pilgrim band was making the round of Jain sacred places in North India. On being asked why they had come on this long pilgrimage, a woman replied: "For the sake of release (*mukti*)," and the gleam on her face showed her devotion.

Modern Jainism shows a tendency to be absorbed by Hinduism. In 1891 the Census reported one and one-half million Jains, but in 1921 there were three hundred thousand less. The three leading Jain sects, Digambara, Svetambara and Sthanakavasi, number each about four hundred thousand souls.

Jainism has made some contribution to the world's thought and life. It is "one of the most emphatic protests the world has ever known against accounting luxury, wealth or comfort, the main things in life."[9] This is the ascetic contribution. On the other hand, most of the money-lending in Western India is in Jain hands. Hence the lay contribution, as stated by the Jain scholar already quoted, is that "Jainism is essentially fitted to give the State good subjects and the country successful business men."[10]

9 Mrs. Stevenson, *op. cit.*, p. 22.
10 Jagmanderlal Jaini, M.A., *op. cit.*, p. 73.

CHAPTER XIII

CHET RAM AND HIS INDIGENOUS CHRISTIAN SECT

THE strange and confused story of Chet Ram shows him successively as a camp-follower of the British army in China, as a Hindu disciple of a Muslim "holy man," as a recipient of a vision of Jesus Christ, and as the founder of an indigenous Christian sect.

Just outside the Taxali Gate, Lahore, in a small garden thickly planted with trees and flowers and trailing vines, stand a tiny square building and several *faqīrs'* huts. The building shelters relics of Chet Ram—his bed and his Bible.

Chet Ram, to whom his followers give the title of *Sain* (Skt. *Svami,* i.e., "Master"), was born at Sharakpur, near Lahore in or about the year 1835 and died in 1894. By caste he belonged to the Aroras, a community of shop-keepers who are found in the south-western Punjab, possibly descended, as Baines[1] thinks, from one of the invading *Shaka* (Scythian) groups. By religion, like his contemporary Keshab Chander Sen, he was originally a Vishnuite. He was not an educated man, knowing apparently only *lunde,* a kind of writing used by shop-keepers. In his *Vision of*

[1] *Ethnography,* p. 33 ff.

Christ he pleads his unfitness for service on account of his ignorance:

> Read I cannot, am unlearned;
> Arabic and Urdu know not.

His disciples too were uneducated. He was an illiterate teacher of illiterate disciples.

Chet Ram was a camp-follower of the British army in China (1858-1860). On his return to India we see him next at Buchhoke, a large village some thirty miles from Lahore. Here lived his father-in-law, a wealthy shop-keeper, and here Chet Ram first met his *guru,* Mahbub Shah. Up to this time Chet Ram had been an idolater. I took down the following account of how he became a disciple of the Muslim ascetic, Mahbub Shah, from the lips of Mor Shah, the keeper of the tombs of Mahbub Shah and Chet Ram at Buchhoke. Mahbub Shah was wandering hither and thither in an abstracted or intoxicated state. Chet Ram had a shop for selling opium and liquor, and as Mahbub Shah passed by would offer him something in the way of a drug or drink. Finally Chet Ram took a bottle of strong drink to the place where Mahbub Shah was stopping, and gave him some of the liquor. Soon after this, the Muslim ascetic, when he was in a drunken state, said: "Fetch me a virgin dish," that is, one never used before. They brought him a clay pot. Mahbub broke the upper part, and the remaining part he filled with the wine that Chet Ram had given him. This Chet Ram drank, and so the bonds of discipleship were forged. From that day Chet Ram abandoned everything and followed Mahbub Shah. So runs the story.

Up to the time of Mahbub Shah's death some three or four years later, Chet Ram devoted himself entirely to him. From all accounts Mahbub Shah was a *Jalali faqīr* belonging to the *Chishti* Muhammadans. The members of the Chishti order are "much given to singing and are generally Shiahs. They worship by leaping up and gesticulating and repeating the name of God, till they work themselves into a frenzy and at last sink down."[2] Mahbub Shah bore the title of Saiyid and was born at Moch in Dera Ismail Khan. He was accustomed always to smack his lips as if he were kissing something. Several miracles are ascribed to him. He died about 1867.

It is reported that for three years Chet Ram haunted the tomb of his spiritual guide, sleeping at night near his bones. One is reminded of the numerous tombs of Chishti Saints in Lahore, which are shrines for popular worship on the part of Muhammadans (and sometimes of Hindus as well). Once I met a former mathematical colleague in College work, a Muhammadan, who was living at a large and splendid *Nakshbandi* tomb near Lahore, meditating day and night and hoping for "visions and revelations."

It was probably at the end of these three years that Chet Ram had his vision of Christ. To him is

2 *Census of the Punjab,* 1881, Vol. I, p. 287.

ascribed the authorship of the poem that contains an account of the vision. The following translation I owe to the late Reverend G. L. Thakur Das, of Lahore:

> Upon the grave of Master Mahbub Shah
> Slept Sain Chet Ram.
>
> A man came in a glorious form,
> Showing the face of mercy.
>
> He called aloud, "Who sleeps there?
> Awake, if thou art sleeping.
>
> Hear these words, O Chet Ram,
> Do this one thing, O *Sundar Sham.*
>
> Build a church on this very spot
> Place the Bible therein.
>
> The learned shall come themselves
> And kiss thy feet."
>
> I realized that it was Jesus God,
> Who appeared in a bodily form.

It is clear that the experience described above was a *dream* for it was night and Chet Ram was sleeping. The figure described in the dream is the figure of the glorified Christ, who draws near to the sleeper, bids him awake, and gives him the command to build a church on that very spot and place the Bible therein. When Chet Ram awoke, he realized that it was "Jesus God" who had appeared in bodily form.

It looks as if Chet Ram had suffered from an inferiority complex. He was almost illiterate, had been a water-carrier or something of the sort in

China, and had been despised and humiliated. As a "compensation for the depressing reality"[3] he doubtless indulged in day-dreaming, seeing his ignorant self elevated as the teacher of learned disciples. What Chet Ram dreamed of, Ramakrishna accomplished.

It is altogether probable that Mahbub Shah had said a good deal to his disciple about Christ. In support of this conjecture I may cite the testimony of the late Reverend Yuhanna Khan, my companion in Chet Rami research, to the effect that his father Ghulam Ghaus, formerly a Muhammadan, had first learned about Christ from a Muhammadan ascetic. Chet Ram may also have learned something about Christ from Christian soldiers in China. Psychologically, we must assume that before Chet Ram had his vision Christ had become for him an object of profound interest. Add to this the nightly vigil at the tomb of his preceptor and the effect of intoxicating drugs. The dream or vision added just the supernatural touch that was needed to convert interest into faith.[4] Thus a Hindu shopkeeper became the disciple of a Muhammadan *faqīr,* and out of this fellowship between *guru* and *chela* was born in the Punjab a purely indigenous Christian sect.

Perhaps the earliest printed reference to Chet Ram and his followers is from the pen of the Reverend

[3] See "Depressed Classes and the Inferiority Complex," by J. C. Heinrich in *The United Church Review,* July 1930, p. 204.
[4] Compare Sadhu Sundar Singh's vision of Christ.

C. W. Forman, D.D. of Lahore in 1879 (some nine years after the "vision"): "One sabbath morning Chet Ram and some of his disciples came to my compound. One of them had been wounded by a boy for saying Christ was Lord. It was touching to see how subdued and quiet they all were, and how much they sympathized with the wounded man, whose head was still bleeding. But it was to his leader he looked chiefly for comfort, who manifested the greatest tenderness towards him. Some of his followers were formerly Hindus, and some Muhammadans, but now they agree in acknowledging Christ as Lord and Saviour." [5]

Some additional statements were appended to the above by the Reverend C. B. Newton to correct "certain erroneous notions and exaggerations": "Chet Ram, with a number of his disciples, came to Lahore, last September, and created a stir in the city by proclaiming himself a Christian. . . . He called on me with sixteen of his disciples, an extraordinary looking set of men. They were stalwart, well-fed fellows, . . . having faces variously expressing the ferocity of brigands, the frenzy of madmen, and the vacancy of idiots. Chet Ram himself is a man . . . of rather pleasing features and serious demeanour. Occasionally, however, he gives way to a sort of excitement or frenzy, which his disciples regard as an indication of divine inspiration. . . . Among his disciples there

[5] Report of the Lahore Station of the Lodiana Mission for 1879, pp. 22-26.

are a few men of respectable appearance and sensible behaviour. . . . Their ideas of Christ and Christianity are crude and vague, some of them asserting that Chet Ram is himsell Christ."

C. B. Newton accompanied Chet Ram back to Buchhoke. On the way "Chet Ram got a beating from the Muhammadan inhabitants of Faizpur for praising Christ. He took it meekly. At Nawan Kot a man who had long been ill came to be healed. Chet Ram tore a rag off his clothes, and gave it to the man, and told him it was given in the name of Christ, who would heal him. . . . One gave him [Chet Ram] a rupee, which he made over to me [C. B. Newton] at once. . . . During my stay I had an opportunity of observing Chet Ram's conduct. . . . He manifests on all occasions a strong feeling of love and reverence for Christ, and undergoes persecution and contumely for His name. . . . One day a total stranger came to the *takya* [Chet Ram's headquarters] and told a story of his sufferings, having been robbed of some article of clothing. Chet Ram at once pulled off his own principal garment and gave it to him. . . . He tells his disciples that they may drink spiritous liquor, but only in moderation. He exhibits so many amiable traits that one cannot help liking him, but on the other hand, he is ignorant, and shows no desire to learn. He likes to hear the New Testament read (not being able to read himself), but says that he does not need instruction from the written word, having it directly from the Holy Spirit and the Twelve Apostles."

A subsequent reference to Chet Ram[6] expresses regret that "he has not laid more stress on the Ten Commandments, some of his followers being respectable men . . . but others of them seeming to revel in all that is low and vile." This vague and ill-considered criticism was most unfortunate, for it led the Government to suspect antinomian tendencies within the Chet Rami sect. As a result a scheme for colonizing that community at *Rakh Madho Das,* near Sharakpur, fell through.

In 1889, in an interview[7] between the late Reverend Talib ud-Din and Sain Chet Ram, answering a question concerning strong drink, Chet Ram justified its use on the ground that it kept the spirit of man in equilibrium. His disciples spoke of him as if he were all in all to them, as if the very existence of God depended on his word.

> There is a God, if Chet Ram says so;
> There is no God, if Chet Ram says no.

This statement is what gave Talib ud-Din the impression that the Chet Rami sect was atheistic, an impression which reappeared in the 1891 Indian Census Report[8] which says, "The followers of Chet Ram . . . are said to deny the existence of God." This erroneous view was corrected in the Census of

[6] Lodiana Mission Report, 1888, pp. 10-11.
[7] *Nur Afshan,* an Urdu Newspaper, Ludhiana, May 23, 1889.
[8] See Section 113 devoted to "Forms of Unbelief."

1901 by the statement that "the sect professes a worship of Christ."

Chet Ram died in 1894 at Buchhoke, and there was cremated. Munshi Nathu tells how his ashes were dissolved in water and swallowed by his enthusiastic disciples, a trait of exaggerated *guru*-worship. Chet Ram appointed his daughter *Budhan Bibi* to succeed him as the head of the sect, although his eldest son Hira Lal was still alive. She is a nun, pledged to life-long celibacy, and, like her father, is very ignorant, although through the efforts of the late Miss Mona Bose and others she has learned to read the Gurmukhi character.

The theology of the Chet Rami sect is found in the Hymn of Chet Ram,[9] a Punjabi poem containing in its original form one hundred lines and in its interpolated form some five hundred. The interpolated portions are the work of Munshi Nathu, the poet and theologian of the sect. Chet Ram's doctrine is rooted in his "Vision of Christ," which constitutes one section of the poem. I here subjoin a metrical version of lines 1-25, 36-43 of the original version. The metre follows the original Punjabi, but the translation is without rhyme.

1. Let me celebrate God's praises
Boundless, filling earth and heaven.

2. All the world hath He created
Why? That all His *name* might cherish.

[9] I succeeded in securing from Munshi Nathu a copy of the Hymn of Chet Ram in Persian Punjabi, which is now in the library of the Forman Christian College, Lahore.

3. From the Name the name was fashioned
From the name the Name discovered.

4. From the Name, charm, spell, enchantment;
Everywhere the name embodied.

5. From the name is known the great Name,
Who of all life is the Giver.

6. From the Name the spirit-world see,
Birth and death in close succession.

7. From the Name came into being
Whatsoever God created.

8. From the Name love was begotten,
From the Name throat-cutting hatred.

9. Through God's *love* man's form was moulded,
And within was placed man's spirit.

10. Through love came the high and lowly;
Through love both to God are pleasing.

11. Through love heaven was exalted,
Through love dust of earth was favored.

12. Through love all good things were given,
Holy men, seers, prophets, sages.

13. *Devi Devata* were given.
Through love, also men and demons.

14. Through love see the world of spirits,
Through love Christ Himself was given.

15. Brother, whom men know as *Jesus,*
None can fully tell His greatness.

16. Christ creator and enjoyer,
In all ages omnipresent.

17. Age by age each incarnation
Is the handiwork of Jesus.

18. All who came as men prophetic,
Jesus sent and then recalled them.

19. *Jesus know to be the true God;*
Heaven and earth are of His splendour.

20. Know the world as God's world, brother;
And this realm the Empress mother's.

21. This is Chet Ram's announcement,
That all men shall be united;

22. He who pointed out a hard path,
He who *harmonized* religions;

23. He who loves a heavy burden,
He who showed salvation's gateway.

24. The Death-angel's host is marching,
Chet Ram hath freed men from it.

25. He it is who entering Kal Yug
Made it seem like unto Sat Yug.

. . . . . .

36. Worldliness forsake, O people,
Do the service of Christ Jesus.

37. With the mouth say "Jesus, Jesus,"
Read the Bible with the Gospels.

38. Build a church in every village,
Sing your songs in every village.

39. Men and women both assemble
In the church to sing God's praises.

40. Christ except there is no refuge
In this world or in the next world.

41. Jesus can the soul deliver;
But without faith no salvation.

42. When Christ sitteth in the judgment,
None can say a word before Him.

43. Ever hold this truth with firmness,
Mary's Son is our foundation.

Throughout the Hymn a central place is given to Jesus. He is a manifestation of the love of God, yea, is the "true God." Every incarnation and prophetic spirit have been sent by Him. People are to confess His name, read the Bible, build churches, and sing His praise. He is the only foundation and refuge, and will finally sit in judgment. As might be expected, there are also traces of Hindu pantheism. From the same ineffable Name come both "love" and "throat-cutting hatred." [10] Next follows the exaltation of Sain Chet Ram. When Jesus appeared to him in vision, He called him *Sundar Sham* (beautiful dark one–an epithet of Krishna), an indication that Chet Ram was to be to India in the nineteenth century what Lord Krishna had been to India in his age. And Chet Ram too, like Keshab Chander Sen, was to be the mediator of a new dispensation, in which all religions would be harmonized and all men united. In answer to the question, "How do the Chet Ramis regard Chet Ram?" Munshi Nathu said, "He is the one through whom we became acquainted

[10] One is reminded of Emerson's stanza in his *Song of the Soul* or *Brahma:*

"Far or forgot to me is near:
Shadow and sunlight are the same,
The vanished gods not less appear,
And one to me are shame and fame."

with the Lord"; another said, "Chet Ram is not dead, but present and works now in the hearts of his followers"; and Mor Shah said, "We regard him as God. He is everything to us." In harmony with this, the Reverend G. L. Thakur Das wrote: "They consider Chet Ram as Christ Himself and claim to have seen Christ in seeing Chet Ram."

The official creed of the Chet Rami sect as translated reads: "Help, O Jesus, Son of Mary, Holy Spirit, Lord God Shepherd. Read the Bible and the Gospels for salvation." The Chet Ramis frequently carry a long rod surmounted by a cross inscribed with the confession of faith. The creed is used practically as a kind of mantra or charm. Yet in the creed there is the recognition of (a) the Holy Trinity consisting of Jesus, the Holy Spirit and God, (b) the Bible as the word of God, and (c) salvation as mediated through the Holy Trinity and made known through the Gospel.

Besides the Christian Trinity there is also another trinity, consisting of *Allah, Parameshwar,* and *Khuda,* the consequence apparently of Chet Ram's attempt to unify the Arabic, Hindu, and Persian points of view and so to "harmonize religions." The three are interpreted, respectively, as Creator, Preserver, and Destroyer, an idea based of course upon the Hindu doctrine of Brahma, Vishnu, and Shiva. *Khuda* is Jesus and He is the Destroyer. The Muslim *Allah* and the Hindu *Parameshwar* have had their day. Now is the turn of Jesus *Khudawand* who will receive the adoration of the whole world. He is mightier than *Allah* and *Parameshwar,* and will destroy their worship; for He is the "true God," the Lord of the *four Yugas,* and the Supreme Ruler over all.

Some form of baptism seems to be the rite of initiation into the sect. Adherents distinguish between internal and external baptism, the baptism of the Holy Ghost and the baptism of water. The baptism of the Spirit is equated with the baptism of the Word, which is described as follows: "When a child is born, then the creed is recited in the ears of the child, and also the names of the Twelve Disciples of Christ." (A novel form of infant baptism!) Four forms of external baptism are also mentioned, baptism with water, earth, air, and fire. *Earth*-baptism takes place when a lay member tears off his clothes, casts dust upon his head, and becomes a monk.

Of these monks and lay members, the former get their food by begging, and are the clergy of the sect. Theoretically, forty monks are always to preach the teaching of Chet Ram. They, like most Indian ascetics, are more or less addicted to the use of intoxicating drugs, such as bhang, charas, opium. They claim that they use such stimulants only to protect themselves from cold and disease.

There does not seem to be any fixed form of religious service. One old Chet Rami monk declared that for the enlightened there is no need of religious wor ship. It is the ordinary *sannyasi* attitude. I invited Munshi Nathu to attend church in Lahore. He replied that all such worship is man-made. Once after a long talk with Munshi Nathu he concluded: "This conversation of ours is worship; no other worship is needed." Ghulam Muhammad, one of the very few literate members of the sect, one day said to me: "I read the Bible every day and especially on the Sabbath." The Chet Rami creed is repeated as an act of worship, and the Hymn of Chet Ram is sometimes chanted. There are also some forms of worship which seem to show the influence of Hinduism and Islam. For example, the relics of Sain Chet Ram are preserved with great care. At evening lighted lamps are placed before the Cross and the Bible. Charms are inscribed with the creed, and with the names of the Twelve Apostles, and hung about the neck. In case of illness the numerical value of the creed (5332) is written on paper, and tied to the arm of the sick, or else made into a pill and swallowed.

The followers of Chet Ram are found only in the Punjab. They are recruited largely from the poorer classes. Caste is observed in the sense that each class of converts takes its food separately.

It is difficult to find out the numerical strength of the sect. Nothing is said in any Census report except that of 1901 (Vol. XVII, p. 117), where we read that "the number of Chet Ram's followers is increasing day by day." This hardly holds true now. Even Ghulam Muhammad, who clearly loves large figures, admits that there has been a "decline in number every day since Chet Ram died." Munshi Nathu's sober estimate (1904) of "less than one thousand Chet Ramis in the whole Punjab" may be taken as sufficiently near the truth. So far as one can judge, the Chet Rami movement has no future. Probably the few hundred members now enrolled will in time disappear, some becoming members of the Christian Church; but some may revert to Hinduism.

To sum up, the Chet Rami sect has the Hindu characteristics of caste, asceticism, and *guru*-worship; it is a *bhakti* movement having its roots in Vaishnavism, Chishti emotionalism, and Christian fervor. Accordingly, it is a synthetic and harmonistic movement with the suggestion of a universalistic program, which aims at unifying Hinduism, Islam, and Christianity.

CHAPTER XIV

SADHU SUNDAR SINGH AND THE RICHES OF SIKHISM

A MAN by birth a Sikh, by conversion a Christian. A man of international experience—having visited Japan, Europe and America—who reminded the West of St. Paul and even of Jesus Christ, who attracted the attention of such scholars as Canon Streeter in England, Professor Heiler in Germany, and Archbishop Söderblom in Sweden. This is Sundar Singh, India's Christian Apostle to the West.

He was born in 1889 in a respectable and well-to-do Sikh family belonging to the Patiala State, Punjab. His mother, who died when he was a lad of fourteen, was the great religious influence in his early life. He gave himself diligently to the study of the Sikh Granth, the Hindu Upanishads and the Muslim Quran, and engaged in meditation for hours at a time. His great longing was to find peace. Through the practice of Yoga under the guidance of a Hindu *sannyasi,* he became able to throw himself into the trance-state and in this way he would gain a temporary peace.

The peace which he sought, however, was to come from another source. In his native village, Rampur, a Christian school had been established by Dr. Wherry. In this school Sundar Singh received a daily lesson in the Christian Scriptures. The Bible fascinated him strangely, especially such words as "Ye shall find rest unto your souls." At the same time it aroused in his mind a fierce resentment. "The religion of the West is false; we must destroy it."[1] In a moment of mad rage he threw the Bible into the fire. Things were clearly headed toward a climax. We are reminded of Saul of Tarsus "breathing threatening and slaughter."

The fateful night of December 17, 1904, had arrived, on which he had even planned self-destruction if peace were not attained. Arising at three o'clock the next morning he took a cold bath and gave himself to prayer, literally wrestling with God and refusing to let go, until a blessing were received, the blessing of *peace*. Then suddenly about half-past five a great light! At first he thought the house was on fire. He went on praying. Soon the cloud of light resolved itself into the figure of a man. He thought it might be Buddha or Krishna, or some other deity. But he heard in Hindustani the words, "Why persecutest thou me? For thee I gave up my life upon the Cross." Then he observed the wound-marks of Jesus of Nazareth. The thought came, "Jesus is not dead but alive, and this is He." Sundar fell down in adoration at His feet. Peace and joy filled him. On

[1] Heiler, *Sadhu Sundar Singh*, p. 24. Prof. Heiler's work is my chief source.

rising the vision was gone, but the peace remained.[2] At once he awoke his father, saying, "I am a Christian. Christ has given me the peace that no other could give."

How shall we interpret this account, which is based on Sundar Singh's own words? Sundar was a psychic. He had already gained through the practice of Yoga the knack of inducing trances, and his whole future life was replete with "visions and revelations."[3] He was an Indian, and as Heiler says, "The Indian spirit is better suited than the European for experiences of vision."[4]

We may compare Sundar Singh's vision of Christ with that of Ramakrishna. The latter's method of "realization" was by way of external imitation or dramatic impersonation. He had a hair-trigger temperament very easily set off into ecstasy and vision. He dressed as Radha and imagined himself as Radha, and so gained a vision of Krishna. He dressed as a Muslim and followed the devotional methods of Islam, and so got a vision of Muhammad. He talked with Christians and read the Bible, and so received a vision of Christ. It meant nothing for Ramakrishna except to give him the feeling that "all religions are true." Very different was the experience of Sundar Singh. In his case there was a keen struggle between a strong objective impression of the radiant person-

[2] Heiler, *op. cit.*, pp. 25-26.
[3] Compare 2 Corinthians XII, 1.
[4] Heiler, *op. cit.*, p. 28.

ality of Christ and the equally strong subjective hatred and antagonism which he felt toward this foreign religion and its founder. It was the same kind of subjective "antinomy" as was probably found in the mind of Saul of Tarsus, when "breathing threatening and slaughter," and at the same time profoundly impressed with the conduct of the martyr Stephen, he journeyed toward Damascus. Something similar once came under my notice at the Sialkot Convention. Mr. Waris ud-Din, an Indian Christian, was reporting the proceedings of the Convention for some newspaper. He was out of sympathy with the Convention as a whole, but at the same time was deeply impressed with the messages given. One morning, as John Hyde was delivering an address, I saw Mr. Waris about to fall to the floor. He was caught in time. Later I heard from his own lips his experience. Three scenes one after another were unrolled before him in the sky: (1) a naked sword stretched out to smite; (2) an uplifted Cross; (3) a multitude of angels praising God. He told his story with profound emotion, and his life received a new direction, which attested the reality of the experience. In like manner, the struggle in the subconsciousness of Saul and something like it in the consciousness of Sundar Singh received their solution through the psychic experience of "vision." In this whole matter we must distinguish between "judgments of fact" and "judgments of value." The psychic facts involved may be left to the investigation of psychologists, but value-judgments must be made by another tribunal. In all three cases mentioned above, the life which resulted from the experience is a standing proof of the spiritual reality of the experience. Heiler rightly urges that we must distinguish in Sundar Singh's vision between the kernel and the husk.[5] The details of the vision and its psychological antecedents belong to the husk. Sundar Singh's tremendous conviction that it was not a fancy, nor a dream, but a reality,[6] has to do with the "kernel," which for him was the reality of the living Christ and the miracle of the divine grace.

Naturally the great change in the life of Sundar was followed by severe testings. He was cast out of his home, a lad of fifteen, and spent the first night—it was cold weather—under a tree, friendless and forsaken, and yet with a wonderful peace in his heart. He referred to it afterwards as his "first night in heaven." [7] Poison had been mixed with his food and he barely escaped death. For a time he was a pupil in the Christian Boys' Boarding School at Ludhiana. From there he was sent to Simla where he was baptized on September 3, 1905, his sixteenth birthday.

As in the experience of Isaiah and Paul, so also in that of Sundar Singh, the time of vision was also the time of a call to service. "Go and bear witness of me" was the word of Christ that rang in his heart.

[5] *Op. cit.*, pp. 29, 31.
[6] Quoted by Heiler, *op. cit.*, p. 27. See also Otto's *The Idea of the Holy*, p. 229.
[7] Heiler, *op. cit.*, p. 34.

Along with it came also to mind the desire of his mother that he would some day become a Sadhu. The two inspirations were combined and the result was the ministry in many lands of Sundar Singh as a Christian Sadhu.

The days of his apprenticeship may be passed over lightly. Clad in the yellow robe of an Indian ascetic he made some tours as a preaching friar, and met incidentally members of the secret *Sannyasi* Mission. For two years he studied in the St. John's Divinity College, Lahore, and for a time was a member of "The Brotherhood of the Imitation" along with Messrs. Stokes[8] and Western. Early in 1913 he attempted a forty-day fast in the jungle, following the example of Christ in the wilderness. Quite likely he was also subconsciously influenced by the great motives of Hindu asceticism. Heiler thinks he completed ten or twelve days of the proposed fast, he himself bearing witness afterwards to the wonderful visions experienced.

Sundar Singh had for some time dreamed of bearing witness in Tibet, that land of mystery to the north. At the age of nineteen he selected it as his special mission field, and made his first journey. Except when further afield in the Far East or in Europe

[8] It was about this time that at one of the Sialkot Conventions, Mr. Stokes, the head of the Brotherhood of the Imitation, accompanied by a young Indian novice—probably Sundar Singh—was greatly distressed at the public confession of sin, so reminiscent of Hawthorne's *Scarlet Letter,* because he feared that the young Indian novice would be utterly disillusioned.

he sought to make one evangelistic tour a year into Tibet. Every trip involved persecution and hardship, as he clambered over the "roof of the world." He was now and then thrown into prison, sometimes under the most terrible conditions. Imprisoned in Nepal in 1914, he wrote in his New Testament, "The presence of Christ has turned my prison into a heaven of blessing."[9] Some of the reports of the Sadhu's experiences in Tibet give trouble to his biographers. That like Paul, the Apostle, and John Paton of the New Hebrides, he had many hair-breadth escapes, is easy to believe. But some accounts, such as that of the ancient *Maharishi* of Kailas, make one pause. Sundar Singh kept no diary. In the case of some of his experiences he, again like Paul, may have been uncertain whether he was "in the body or out of the body."[10]

Beginning with 1912 the sphere of Sundar Singh's witness-bearing was enlarged to cover the whole of India and also the regions of the Far East, Burma, the Straits Settlements, Japan, and China. He drew India as a magnet,[11] and not only Christians, but also Hindus and Muhammadans hung upon his words. He had reached the zenith of his influence. Naturally it was a time of temptation. The thought could not but suggest itself of a syncretism of the great religions of the world, Hinduism, Islam, Buddhism, and

[9] Heiler, *op. cit.*, p. 55.
[10] 2 Corinthians XII, 2.
[11] Macnicol, *Making of Modern India*, 1924.

Christianity, with himself as the teacher and herald of the new world movement. For it is the ambition of every great religious personality of India to found a special movement and become its head. The temptation was met and overcome and the memorial of his spiritual victory is found in his booklet, *At the Feet of the Master.*

The trip to the Far East was followed in 1920 by a visit to Europe and America. His aim was to bear witness, and incidentally to find out at first hand the spiritual condition of the West. Sundar Singh's father, who had followed his son in Christian faith, furnished the funds for two journeys abroad. Both were made in triumph, the first covering Great Britain, America and Australia, and the second Palestine, France, Switzerland, Germany, Norway, Sweden, Denmark, and Holland. In Stockholm Sundar Singh was the guest of Prince Oscar Bernadotte and in Copenhagen he called on the former Russian Czarina in the royal palace.

Everywhere in Europe, America, and Australia the Sadhu received an enthusiastic welcome. The West had been sending Christian missionaries to India. Now there came from India a Christian Indian to preach the gospel to the West. He impressed people as resembling a Biblical character. Through him primitive Christianity was made real. His voice seemed like the voice of "a man from another world." For many his preaching was a spur to a new Christian life. Thus his visit to Europe was an "event." His visit, however, resulted in profound disillusionment. He found the West as a whole spiritually unfaithful to the light it had received, with a shallow religious life lacking in inwardness and soul culture. There was not only disillusion, but also danger. He, an Indian, was reverenced as a saint by Europeans, and he had met and mingled on easy terms with some of the royalty of Europe. One can readily understand that it was the time of the greatest temptation of his life. He ran the danger of taking to himself the praise which he knew belonged to his Master Christ alone.

Professor Heiler says truly that the life of Sundar Singh reads like that of one of the saints described in the *Acta Sanctorum* of the Roman Church, or in the Hindu *Bhakta-Mala.*[12] The first place in his *vita contemplativa* was given to prayer, and on this he put a tremendous emphasis. At the time of his conversion he was praying, and his testimony is that "all he had ever found, he had gained through prayer alone." [13] He rebuked the West for being prayerless, and so losing the sense of God, since "it is only to the one who prays that the spiritual life becomes a reality." [14] His mother taught him to pray, and there had been the daily use of the *Japji*. Thus Sundar Singh brought with him into the Christian Church the riches of Sikh devotion, to be further enriched by the example and teaching of Jesus Christ. The

12 Heiler, *op. cit.*, p. 75.
13 Heiler, *op. cit.*, p. 76.
14 Heiler, *op. cit.*, p. 79.

prayers of Sundar Singh, like those of John Hyde, were times of communion with a Heavenly Friend, when the longing was not so much for gifts as for the presence of the Giver of gifts.[15] In his prayers the Sadhu sometimes used language reminiscent of the Upanishads, as, e.g., "Life of my life and Spirit of my spirit." [16] "His way of prayer was quite that of the Catholic mystics." [17] We are reminded constantly of Augustine, St. Francis, and Thomas à Kempis, and of *The Imitation of Christ,* as well as of the Sufi mystics of Islam. "The Sadhu belongs," says Heiler, "to the greatest of Christian men of prayer."

As in the case of the great mystics there is a scale of experiences, rising from meditation through speechless contemplation and issuing in ecstasy, so was it with Sundar Singh. For him ecstasy was "a precious gift of God," a source of spiritual insight, a means of strength for his ministry, and a foretaste of the joy of heaven. Sundar Singh's experiences throw light upon the "visions and revelations" of the prophets and apostles of the Bible.

Peace is the deepest longing of the Oriental soul. The ordinary salutation is *"Salam!"* (Peace!), and the

[15] Heiler, *op. cit.,* pp. 81, 83, 87.

[16] Heiler, *op. cit.,* p. 89.

[17] The fact that the Sadhu was not a member of the Catholic Church, and at the same time seemed to possess the marks of a Catholic saint, has been variously interpreted by Catholics. For the Jesuit Hosten, the Sadhu, not being a Catholic, must necessarily be a fraud; but for a French Catholic scholar, the Sadhu was a "new St. Paul," who was sent to "the heathen of heresy," that is, to the Protestants, to prepare them for a return to the Catholic fold. See Heiler, pp. viii and 244.

Brahmanical benediction is *"Om! shanti, shanti, shanti!"* (Peace, peace, peace!)[18] It was Sundar Singh's unutterable longing for peace which prepared him for receiving at his conversion "the peace of God which passeth all understanding." This peace was for him the central miracle and proof of Christianity. It was, as he testified, a continuous experience of his Christian life, but deepened in times of special persecution and in moments of ecstasy.

Sundar Singh followed the ways of Indian asceticism as far as the yellow robe, occasional fasting and great simplicity of life are concerned, but he inflicted upon himself no artificial torments, such as hook-swinging, lying on a bed of spikes, or self-mutilation. Suffering enough came to him as he preached Christ in Tibet, some of it extreme.[19] He brought to the attention of the West the simplicity and other worldliness and spirituality of the best type of Indian asceticism.

His oft-repeated expression, "Heaven on earth," seems to be an echo of a passage in one of the Upanishads,[20] but the thought is based upon the New Testament. He experienced in the fellowship of Christ a bit of "heaven" even in the midst of great affliction, as on that night under the tree after he had been cast out from home, or when in Tibet he had been thrown into a pit full of dead men's bones.

[18] I recall the impressive way in which Swami Vivekananda uttered this threefold benediction at the end of his address in Lahore.
[19] Heiler, *op. cit.*, pp. 52-56.
[20] *Chhandogya Upanishad,* II, 3, 3.

The richness of the Sadhu's "contemplative life" was matched by the equal richness of his "active life." The one was the preparation for the other; the contemplative finding its fruition in the active. We are reminded of a similar balance in the life of John Hyde, as well as in the life of the Hindu world-figure, Swami Vivekananda, who in so many ways represented a new and practical type of Hindu ascetic life.

So the mystic and ecstatic was also the tireless worker. From the writings of Guru Nanak, the founder of Sikhism, Sundar Singh had learned in his boyhood that religion consists in the fear of God and in the doing of good works.

As a Christian, Sundar Singh stressed witness-bearing through lips, through life, and also through death. Something of the "lion-like" strength of the early Sikh martyr, Guru Arjun, was in his makeup, and so for him one of the attractions of Tibet as a sphere of work lay in the possibility of one day suffering martyrdom there.

Another principle of Sundar Singh, "In the world but not of the world," was also voiced by Guru Nanak in almost the same words, "Though in the world, I am not of the world." The Sadhu clarified this thought by wonderful illustrations.

His was the theology of experience rather than of reflection. For him Christianity is "no book religion, but a religion of life," [21] and its true teachers

[21] Heiler, *op. cit.*, p. 118.

are the "specialists" in the Christian life—men of prayer, prophets, mystics. Sundar Singh was a master in the use of illustrations taken from life. His speech, like that of a child, was simple, concrete, pictorial. Heiler calls him a "child." [22]

Sundar Singh in his conception of God showed the influence of his Hindu background. The unknown "abyss" of the divine nature as conceived by Neo-Platonism and Vedantic mysticism, reappears in the Sadhu's thought as still the "incomprehensible" and the "unutterable," but at the same time viewed as personalized Love, after the manner of the *bhakti* mysticism of India and the Christian mysticism of the West. He even applied to God the favorite Indian expression, "Ocean of Love," and quite after the Indian fashion called God "Our Spiritual Mother." [23] He apparently rejected the ordinary Christian view of an external world-judgment at the last day, and proclaimed an immanent, automatic, and impersonal judgment, the sinner judged by his own sin,[24] after the manner of the Hindu doctrine of Karma. "The peace of God which passeth all understanding" was the revelation in the experience of Sundar Singh of "the God of peace," the *Deus semper quietus* of Mysticism. Thus something of the quiet and calm which are ascribed to the Brahma of

22 Heiler, *op. cit.*, p. 117.
23 Heiler, *op. cit.*, p. 123.
24 Compare John III, 17 ff. and Heiler, p. 126.

the Upanishads and the Nirvana of the Buddhists belongs also to Sundar Singh's conception of God.[25]

God's nature being love, the motive of creation must be the love of God. The visible world of nature is an image or copy of the invisible world of spirit. Hence for Sundar Singh, as for Saint Francis, everything in nature has a mystic and spiritual significance. Both could speak of their little brothers and sisters, the birds. I once heard Sundar Singh tell this story. He was in Tibet. A tree which held in its branches a nest of young birds had caught fire. The mother bird flew round and round in a distracted manner, but finally settled down on her nest, spread her wings over her young and perished with them. It is not difficult to imagine the application which the Sadhu made.[26]

Sundar Singh is for his generation a revelation of the spiritual depth and inwardness, and of the tremendous "driving power"[27] of primitive Christianity. Hence in very truth a creative religious personality. Like his Master, Christ, he came "not to destroy, but to fulfil," not to cast away *in toto* his old spiritual inheritance, but carefully to separate the gold from the dross, so as to take with him into

[25] Heiler, *op. cit.*, p. 127.

[26] See also Heiler, *op. cit.*, p. 138.

[27] In his restless energy the Sadhu reminds us of St. Paul. He dreamed of going to Tibet, just as Paul dreamed of going to Spain (Rom. XV, 24-28). He selected that difficult field, where little or no evangelistic work was done, so as not to build on "another man's foundations" (Rom. XV, 20). The same driving energy sent him to Europe and America.

Christianity the "riches of Sikhism." He believed that all that is good and true and beautiful in any religion is a *præparatio evangelica* for still better things, even for the Gospel of Jesus Christ. As Swami Vivekananda, India's Hindu apostle to the West, held that Vedantism is the fulfilment of all the religions of the world, so Sundar Singh held that the religion of Christ is the "Crown" [28] and fulfilment of the aspirations of every religion. Accordingly the best aspirations and habitudes of all religions are sacred things, to be handled reverently, since they not only contain truth, but as such are the foundation of anything higher. It is a question then of faithfulness to light received. This is the point of the Sadhu's stern prophetic rebuke to the West: "Indians are more faithful to the light they have than you are to the light you have. Through the pressure of external and material things you of the West are allowing the sense of God and the practice of prayer to be crowded out."

In midsummer of 1930 Sundar Singh made his last tour into Tibet. He has never returned. Somewhere upon "the roof of the world" the Sadhu has "fallen on sleep," perishing perhaps of cold or receiving the crown of martyrdom, no one, as in the case of Moses, knowing "of his sepulchre unto this day."

[28] Compare the title of the late Dr. J. N. Farquhar's book, *The Crown of Hinduism.*

CHAPTER XV

DR. KURTKOTI AND HIS PROCESSION OF NAKED SADHUS

THERE is no respect in which orthodox Hinduism stands in sharper contrast with other religions than in its reverence for religious nakedness. In no other country in the world is it conceivable that nakedness should be a sign of holiness.

I was present in 1918 at the Kumbh Mela which is held every twelfth year[1] at the junction of the two sacred rivers, Ganges and Jumna, just below Allahabad. Over a million people were present, pilgrims from all parts of India, and the heads of the ascetic orders with their followers, sadhus of every name in large numbers. There were many present who could converse fluently in Sanskrit. I ventured into one meeting where the head of some religious community and his followers were assembled. Their speech was all in Sanskrit. Both the ascetic discipline of India and its sacred scholarship were well represented. In fact, it was a kind of "General Assembly" of Hinduism. The Nagas, or "naked ascetics," were present in full force, and I watched for a few moments what

[1] Farquhar, *Outline of the Religious Literature of India*, p. 174.

probably was the *Diksha,* or "initiation" of a young man into this order.

The crowning event of "the great day of the feast" was the procession of the Nagas for a half mile or more down to the junction of the sacred rivers to take a ceremonial bath. Their line of march was roped off, in order to keep back the crowds. Armed with a camera, I drew near the rope. The procession had not yet started. I ventured to get inside for a better view. At once some one accosted me with the words, "Would you not like to meet His Holiness Shri Shankaracharya?" "Certainly," I replied. I was immediately escorted to "His Holiness" who was seated in a palanquin at the head of the procession, in readiness for the start. His full title is "Jagadguru Shri Shankaracharya of Karvir Pith," and he is the present-day *Mahant* of one of the four original monasteries founded by the great Shankaracharya in the eighth century, A.D. He is one of the heads, if not the chief head, of orthodox Hinduism. Dr. Kurtkoti had a pleasing address, spoke English well, told me that he had received the degree of Ph.D. from an American university, and was examiner in Sanskrit for the Bombay University. He permitted me to take his picture. His home is in Kolhapur, Western India, where he is the domestic chaplain of the Maharaja of Kolhapur. It was he that officiated at the wedding of Sir Takaji Rao Holkar, ex-Maharaja of Indore, and Miss Nancy Anne Miller of Seattle, Washington.

His secretary, Pundit Dev Ratan, who soon made himself known to me, proved to be an old acquaintance of mine in Lahore. For many years he had been the secretary of Pundit S. N. Agnihotri of the Deva Samaj, and my acquaintance with him in those days had been enlivened by some friendly controversy. He had broken his connection with Pundit Agnihotri and tried to found a new religious society, but had not been successful. It was something of a jump from the secretaryship of Agnihotri and his "science-grounded" religion to the service of His Holiness of Karvir Pith and his naked Sadhus.

The procession started. A great crowd of men, women, and children pressed on the ropes from both sides. Headed by the palanquin in which "His Holiness" was carried, the Naga ascetics, two by two, as naked as the day they were born, walked in solemn procession down to the bathing place. Needless to say, I took plenty of snapshots, *nemone contradicente.* The ascetics walked as in a dream, their faces straight ahead.

I was interested to note the reaction of the spectators. Every face was intent and solemn. When the procession had passed, men and women rushed into the empty space between the ropes, and lifted the sand that had been pressed by sacred feet, throwing it over their heads, their faces revealing their ecstatic mood. For them it was as it were a high sacrament—the sacrament of the nakedness of holy men.

What is the explanation of this curious ritual? For

one thing the climate of India not only permits nudity, in fact, at certain seasons the intense heat encourages nudity. Only in a hot climate could such a religious custom have started. The Naga ascetics are not a tribe or a sect, the name Naga [2] being used only to designate such Vaishnava Vairagis and Shaiva *Sannyasis* as have carried their renunciation to the point of dispensing with clothes. Of course, they are not permitted by the Indian Government to go about naked in public places, although once I saw an entirely naked Sadhu just outside Jhansi, walking toward the city (soon to be stopped by the police). In their own monastic quarters and at religious festivals like the Kumbh Mela they are permitted to appear naked. There are women Nagas also, but the good sense of India demands proper clothing for them. In fact, during the Kumbh Mela, when hundreds of Sadhus marched in absolute nudity, the rear of the procession was brought up by some dozens of clothed Naga Sadhvis. Between men ascetics and women ascetics there is thus a "double standard" as regards modesty.

Religious nudity is supposed to imply on the part of the naked ones an entire lack of self-consciousness such as is found in very young children. That strange personality, Ramakrishna, is represented by his biographers as in his transcendent moods unable

[2] "Many of the Dasanamis have discarded clothing and are called Nagas (from *Nagna* 'naked'). There were hundreds of them at the Kumbh Mela of 1918." Farquhar's *Outline*, 1920, p. 174, n. 1.

to keep his "cloth" in place, moods during which he in his innocence and lack of self-consciousness was "like a child." [3] To those Hindus who watched with reverence the procession of naked Sadhus at the Kumbh Mela, the dominant thought must have been that these holy men were so engrossed in transcendent and eternal verities that they had no consciousness of such a finite and mundane thing as nakedness. To the onlookers, then, it was a procession of those who had "received the Kingdom of heaven *as a little child*." [4]

Religious nudity stands in vital relation to *sannyasa* (renunciation). Ordinary Hindu renunciation involves the surrender of parents, wife, children, home, friends, name, caste, property and almost all clothes. We see, however, occasional instances of the working of a certain logical ruthlessness, which not infrequently characterizes Hinduism. If the surrender of some clothes is good, then the surrender of all clothes must be better. If the cutting off of the accessories of life is good, then the cutting off of life itself through voluntary starvation, as sometimes occurs in Jainism, must be better. In no other country in the world have ideas such terrific force as in India.

[3] See Wendell Thomas, *Hinduism Invades America*, p. 63.

[4] The general presupposition of non-religious nudity is also lack of self-consciousness as observed not only in very young children, but also in primitive tribes living in a hot climate. One may cite from the Hebrew story (Gen. II, 25; III, 7-11) the case of Adam and Eve, who in the days of their innocence were naked and "unashamed." There are in these modern days Nudist colonies, ostensibly for hygienic purposes, sun baths, etc. But the procession of naked Sadhus at the Kumbh Mela was a religious ritual.

As an incentive to religious nudity there is also the force of ideal or actual example. Shiva is "the chief patron god of ascetics, and Shiva is represented as *digambara*"[5] (sky-clad, or naked). Mahavira, great teacher of Jainism, though reared in Kshatriya comfort, asserted his independence even of clothes, and has been followed in this custom by the Jain sect of the "sky-clad." The example of Totapuri, "the naked one," may have made it easier for Ramakrishna, his disciple, to drop his cloth at times and to lapse into nakedness.

Religious nudity may also be taken as an illustration of one of the fundamental doctrines of philosophical Hinduism. A distinction is drawn between Brahman with attributes and Brahman without attributes. Clothed with attributes, it is the "lower Brahman," and belongs to the sphere of *maya*. Unclothed, it is the "higher Brahman," complete Reality untouched by *maya*, concerning which not a single affirmation may legitimately be made. Thus the ascetic devoid of clothing is in best harmony with the doctrine of the Brahman devoid of attributes.

It was Totapuri, the naked ascetic from the Punjab, who taught Ramakrishna the doctrine of the unqualified Brahman.

[5] See Geden, *Asceticism—Hindu*, E.R.E., II, 93.

CHAPTER XVI

PANDITA RAMABAI AND THE HINDU HERITAGE

It was in 1908 that I met Pandita Ramabai at her Home for Widows and Orphans at Kedgaon, Western India. As the head of a great religious and philanthropic institution with some two thousand young people under her care, she impressed me as one of the most wonderful women I had ever seen. She was a Christian, having come by slow stages out of Hinduism, bringing with her, as was natural, some of the habits, methods, and points of view of her old religious life. A sketch of her career will indicate some of the things she owed to her Hindu heritage.

Ramabai was born near Mangalore in 1858, daughter of Anant Shastri Dungre and his second wife, Lakshmibai, both Chitpawan Brahmans.[1] It was a

[1] The Chitpawans are one of the twelve divisions of the Maharashtra Brahmans, their original habitat being the Konkan. For a hundred years (up to 1818) a Chitpawan family furnished Peshwas, or prime ministers, to the Maratha state. Among famous Chitpawans of later days may be mentioned Mahadev Govind Ranade, founder of the modern social movement, Gopal Krishna Gokhale, far-seeing statesman of the last generation, Bal Gangadhar Tilak, Vedic scholar and popular leader, the Reverend Nilkant Nehemiah Goreh, Sanskrit scholar and convert to Christianity, Narayan Vaman Tilak, poet and Christian, and Pandita Ramabai. Instead of brown eyes, the almost invariable rule in India, Ramabai

case of child marriage, Anant Shastri being 44 years old and Lakshmibai 9. Of the six children of the second marriage, three died in childhood.

Ramabai's father, Anant, had abandoned the non-dualistic Vedanta of Shankara and embraced Vaishnavite *bhakti* (loving devotion to God). *Bhakti* in Hinduism, as Dr. Macnicol remarks,[2] has "its parallel in the evangelical fervours of emotional Christianity." It was this religious attitude that Ramabai inherited from her early home life. She brought "the glory and honour" of her Hindu heritage into the Christian Church.

Ramabai's father showed a zeal for education. He had gained the title of *Shastri,* as the pupil of a learned Brahman at Poona who was engaged contrary to all custom in teaching Sanskrit to a woman, the wife of Baji Rao, the last of the Peshwas. Anant Shastri caught the idea from his preceptor and determined that his wife Lakshmibai should also be

had grey eyes, a characteristic of not a few Chitpawans. Hence the theory held by some that the Chitpawans are descended from foreigners wrecked on the Konkan shore. There was commercial intercourse between Babylon and Western India as early as 800 B.C. and possibly even earlier.

2 *Pandita Ramabai,* 1926, p. 4. On the occasion of my visit to Mukti in 1908 I was present one morning in the great hall during a devotional service. The meeting began quietly with one or two brief talks and with the singing of hymns. Next came a stirring address from one of the voluntary foreign workers and a call to prayer. It was the signal for an extraordinary outburst. Nearly one fourth of the two thousand present—most or all of them young women—began to pray audibly, bodies swaying and heads jerking, transformed for the time being literally into "Quakers" and "Shakers." The shaking was so violent in many cases that their hair was loosened and whipped around their heads. Meanwhile, Pandita Ramabai sat quietly, neither urging nor checking.

taught the sacred tongue. It caused such opposition among the relatives, however, that Anant and his wife took refuge in the Gangamula Forest, where at last Lakshmibai got her chance to learn Sanskrit. There an *Ashram* was established to which students came from far and near. In all this Anant showed great strength of character, and Lakshmibai was a true helpmate, showing executive ability in the management of the *Ashram* and even assisting in the teaching of Sanskrit.

This idyllic condition was not to continue. The folly and fraud of Anant's relatives brought about his financial ruin, and he had to leave his forest home and seek some new means of livelihood. Ramabai at this time was only a few months old.

Now followed twenty years (1858-1878) of homeless wandering over the length and breadth of India, years of suffering. As Dr. Macnicol writes, "This school of suffering was Pandita Ramabai's university. . . . She comes forth a graduate in life, in its wisdom and calm judgment." [3] From the age of eight to fifteen Ramabai was taught by her mother, and the Vaishnava scriptures *Bhagavadgita* and *Bhagavata Purana* were committed to memory in Sanskrit. For a time the father gained a comfortable living by reading and expounding the Puranas. At Dwarka by the sea they stayed a whole year, since it was a specially holy Vaishnava shrine. All the while Rama-

[3] *Pandita Ramabai,* p. 12.

bai's brother, Shrinivasa, engaged in prayers and austerities, worshipping especially Hanuman the Monkey god, but nothing unusual happened. So they tried another Hanuman temple near Madras. Their money was now gone, and days of famine (1873) were beginning. Within a few months of one another Ramabai's father, mother, and sister all died of starvation. Before his death Anant said to Ramabai, "I have given you into God's keeping . . . and you must always serve Him." So Anant Shastri and Lakshmibai his wife fell by the way, their lives testifying throughout to the strength and ardor in the pursuit of God of the Hindu soul. Sad and disillusioned, Ramabai and her brother Shrinivasa came in 1878 to Calcutta, the center of the reform movements.

Ramabai was marked off from other Hindu women by certain characteristics. She was at the age of twenty unmarried, in spite of Gautama's injunction that "a girl should be given in marriage before puberty."[4] She was also learned in Sanskrit lore, and as such was a "new woman." She met Keshab Chander Sen, who advised her to study the Vedas and Upanishads. About the same time an assembly of Sanskrit scholars in Calcutta gave Ramabai the title of *Sarasvati*,[5] so far as I know the first and only in-

[4] *Gautama Dharma-Sutra*, XVIII, 21-23; S.B.E., II, 269.

[5] *Sarasvati* (modern Sarsuti) is the name of a stream in the Eastern Punjab, now dry most of the year, along the banks of which probably for generations the Vedic clans had their center, and where many of the hymns of the Rigveda must have been com-

stance of the bestowal upon a woman of this title in modern India. Hence she was called *Pandita.*

Ramabai was indignant at the disability under which Hinduism[6] places women, in that as women they are not able to attain directly to *Mukti* (release), but must await reincarnation as men. She had in her the same spirit of reform that characterized Ram Mohan Roy and Keshab Chander Sen. In 1880 Shrinivasa died and Ramabai was left alone. She showed her strength and independence as a reformer by the marriage of herself, a Chitpawan Brahman, with Bipin Beharidas Medhavi, a Bengali Shudra. To be sure, he was an educated man, possessing the degrees M.A. and LL.B., and had studied in a mission school. After nineteen months of happy married life he died of cholera, leaving a little daughter Manoramabai.

It was about this time that Ramabai had her first contacts with Christianity. She had attended a Christian social meeting with her brother before his death —where a copy of the Bible (or a portion of it) in Sanskrit had been given to her; and several times she had met a Baptist missionary at Silchar.

The widowed Ramabai and her daughter went to Poona, the headquarters of the Chitpawans. Her

posed. Hence "the river of wisdom," and later "wisdom" itself. As a title bestowed for excellence in Sanskrit scholarship it was gained by Swami Dayananda Sarasvati and Pandita Ramabai Sarasvati.

[6] That is to say, according to the popular view of what Hinduism teaches.

linguistic equipment at this time consisted of Marathi, Hindustani, and Bengali, as well as Sanskrit, and she was determined to learn English. She founded the *Arya Mahila Samaj,* a club for Indian women, and worked hard against child-marriage and ignorance. She attacked fiercely the evils tolerated in Hinduism, being sometimes almost as strong in her statements as Katherine Mayo. Naturally this provoked antagonism, which expressed itself at times in malicious gossip, of which the following is a specimen: "The horrid creature, when her father had duly and properly married her to Sri Krishna at Dwarka, must needs commit sacrilege and marry a Bengali Babu."

During the years 1883-1885 Ramabai and her daughter were in England. She had raised funds for the voyage by writing *Morals for Women.* She studied at the Cheltenham Ladies' College, and, Chitpawan-like, translated her dream of learning English into reality. In 1883, while living with the Wantage Sisters of the Church of England, she and her daughter were baptized.

Next we see Pandita Ramabai in America (1886-1888), where she wrote *The High Caste Hindu Woman,* a book which made a tremendous appeal, and was the cause of the formation of many "Ramabai Associations" in America. Ramabai was reckoned by Max Müller as one of the pioneers in Indian reform. Through her experiences in England and

America she was becoming internationally minded, and in her book on *Social Conditions in America* she seemed to foresee the advent of Prohibition and International Peace.

Ramabai returned to India in 1889 and plunged at once into social and philanthropic work—a widow opening for widows the *Sharada Sadan* [7] (Home of Wisdom) in Bombay. She received the cordial support of the Bombay and Poona leaders of social reform, M. G. Ranade, K. P. Telang, R. G. Bhandarkar and N. G. Chandawarkar, but was opposed by Bal Gangadhar Tilak, the representative of conservatism. In the Home the widows were free to follow the religious practices of their faith, but the Christian influence of Ramabai, even though she said nothing, was strong. A storm of opposition broke over her in 1893, for it was found that of the fifty-three girls in the Home, twenty were in the habit voluntarily of attending Ramabai's daily prayers. M. G. Ranade, Dr. Bhandarkar and others resigned their membership on the Advisory Committee.

The course of Ramabai's spiritual pilgrimage should now be summarized. In the Calcutta days she was a Brahmo theist. At Wantage, in 1883, she intellectually accepted Christianity and was baptized. While in America, she was spiritually becalmed,

[7] *Sharada* means "wisdom." The "*Sharada* script" is used in Kashmir, and the wife of Ramakrishna bore the name *Sharada Devi.*

making no progress. But after her return to India in 1891 she underwent a deeper religious experience stimulated by Mr. Haslam's *From Death to Life,* and by the addresses of Dr. Pentecost, Mr. Gregson, and Robert Wilder. No wonder the storm broke in 1893, for she now possessed new life and joy and power. In 1895 twelve of the girls in the *Sharada Sadan* were baptized as Christians. Dressed as a religious beggar, Ramabai that same year visited Brindaban in order to see at first-hand the condition of the Hindu widows there.

The great famine of 1896-1899 reminded Ramabai vividly of her earlier experiences. There rang in her ears the words, "Who knoweth whether thou are not come to the kingdom for such a time as this?" [8] Again, to find out the facts, she went to Bundelkhand, as she had gone before to Brindaban. She saw with her own eyes the horrors of the famine and the "trade in young girls." She determined to save three hundred girls of any and every caste.

It was a time of ferment and change. She read voraciously. Among the books that impressed Ramabai were *Story of the China Inland Mission, The*

[8] Esther IV, 14. I recall once at the Sialkot Convention that Esther's decision "to go in unto the king, which is not according to the law," and her saying, "If I perish, I perish" (Esther IV, 16), were the subject of a morning's devotional meditation. A leading Indian Christian arose and with passionate eloquence reminded the women present of Esther's example in doing for the sake of country and God things "not according to law" and custom. Many women of India have recently gone the way of Esther, greatly daring for the sake of country and God.

Lord's Dealings with George Müller, and *The Life of John G. Paton, Founder of the New Hebrides Mission.* An outbreak of plague forced the transfer of the Home from Bombay and Poona to the village Kedgaon. The rural surroundings here were very like the *Ashram* in the Gangamula Forest, where Ramabai was born. "She was henceforth almost as completely confined within the boundaries of Mukti as if she had been a Mother Abbess within her convent walls."[9] Earlier the inmates of the Home had been Hindu widows of good caste, but now three hundred girls of every caste were received, many of them wild and undisciplined. The chief end became their salvation. At an earlier period the Home was *Sharada Sadan,* "Place of Learning"; now it was *Mukti Sadan,* "Place of Salvation." Henceforth Ramabai's work lay among the poor and weak and despised. It was a demonstration that India needed far beyond anything else—a demonstration of the preciousness of human personality.

In 1898 Ramabai made a second visit to America. She gave an account of her stewardship and secured promises of help for the future. On her return to India, in the same year, the work at Kedgaon was

[9] Macnicol, *Pandita Ramabai,* p. 103. In 1908, at the suggestion of Mary Borden, the novelist, I called on Pandita Ramabai at Kedgaon to persuade her, if possible, to go forth and bear her Christian testimony in the chief cities of India, as she had done in 1886 at Poona, "the intellectual capital of India." She did not consent. She felt that her work lay among the two thousand or more gathered at Mukti, who were under her own immediate influence.

divided into three departments, educational, philanthropic, and spiritual. As a philanthropic activity, she founded a rescue home which soon had three hundred inmates.

The great famine was especially terrible in Gujrat in 1899. In 1896 Ramabai had visited Bundelkhand alone. Now, on the same errand of mercy, she sent out twenty of her helpers, of whom eight had been rescued from starvation in 1896. The result was that by 1900 Mukti had a population of nineteen hundred to provide for. An industrial department was added, and voluntary helpers from many lands—England, America, Sweden, Australia, New Zealand—joined Ramabai's force. The same year Manoramabai finished her studies in England and America and returned to India to help her mother.

The human material gathered at Mukti was very raw, gross, and superstitious. Many girls claimed to be possessed by evil spirits. A special prayer-circle was formed in 1905 to pray for a revival, and before long the revival came. It was accompanied by physical manifestations as in the early religious revivals of America, such as shaking and quivering, and sensations of burning, the loud clamor of simultaneous prayer, and "speaking with tongues." The breath from heaven helped to cleanse the fetid air. Those who had been spiritually transformed needed to express their new life in service. To this end "prayer-bands" were established, each band of young women chaperoned by an elderly woman, and ready to receive invitations to do evangelistic work outside.[10]

Pandita Ramabai was not satisfied with the current translation of the Bible into Marathi. She feared that the use of certain terms might convey the Vedantic philosophy, and also that the whole was tainted with the "higher criticism." She determined therefore to provide a version herself. As a linguistic preparation for this task she had learned some Hebrew and Greek. For the translation of the Old Testament she secured assistance from the *Beni-Israel,* a Jewish community on the western coast. Her version, as far as it went, was composed, printed, and bound by the women of Mukti, and was distributed gratis.

In 1919 Pandita Ramabai received the Kaiser-i-Hind gold medal from the King-Emperor, George V. She died on April 5, 1922.

How did Ramabai's "Hindu heritage" color her Christian life? The Hindu emphasis on meditation and prayer never ceased to be hers. Like Mahatma Gandhi she got up at four o'clock in the morning for

[10] I was once at an evening preaching service in Kodoli, near Kolhapur. The veranda of the local dispensary served as pulpit. After some ordinary speaking a young man addressed the crowd with great earnestness. I made inquiries later and learned his story from himself. Some years before he had been a "nominal" Christian. One of Pandita Ramabai's prayer-bands was in the place at that time, and had gone out with the pastor and others to a village near by for an evangelistic service. The young man followed, determined to have some fun. He was jeering, when suddenly he found himself surrounded by the young women of the prayer-band, who were on their knees praying for him. Before he knew it, he also was upon his knees.

her devotions, and she never allowed the pressure of other work to interfere with her times of meeting with God. But of course the same lesson is taught by the example of Christ. At this point Hindu and Christian ideals coalesce.

As a widow Ramabai accepted the position assigned by Hindu custom to widows. No ornaments, close clipped hair, the dress of Hindu widowhood, a vegetarian diet, and extreme toil, her day beginning at four A.M. and never seeming to end. But the toil which to ordinary widows in India is often drudgery was to Ramabai her glory and joy, for it was on behalf of the "little ones" for whom Christ died. Ramabai demonstrated that India's widows will be an asset, and not a liability, when they are emancipated and educated and regenerated.

As a woman Ramabai proved the value for India and for the world of the education of India's women. She showed that a woman, nay a widow, could merit the title of "Builder of India."[11] She thus stands as a modern analogue of the famous women of ancient India, such as Sita and Damayanti.

Ramabai had the religious creativeness and the instinct for leadership of the noblest members of the Brahman community. Chitpawan scholarship and Chitpawan administrative ability reappear in her. She certainly brought something of "the glory and honor" of the Hindu spiritual heritage into the

11 Dr. Macnicol's *Pandita Ramabai* belongs to the "Builders of Modern India" series.

Christian church. No wonder, then, that at a memorial meeting after her death Mrs. Sarojini Naidu, the Hindu poetess, laid claim to Ramabai in behalf of Hinduism as "the first Christian to be enrolled in the calendar of Hindu saints."

CHAPTER XVII

JOHN N. HYDE AND THE WAYS OF HINDU MEDITATION

DR. HARRY EMERSON FOSDICK has remarked, "There is no possibility of Indian religion escaping the influence of Jesus Christ, and there is no possibility of American religion escaping the influence of the great Indian faiths." [1] Numerous illustrations of the religious impact of the West upon India have been given, as well as of the contrary process through the lectures especially of Swami Vivekanand and Swami Ram. The choicest things of Hinduism have also influenced Christian missionaries. Some have been known to don the yellow robe for longer or shorter periods, notably Messrs. Stokes and Western; and the methods of the Hindu *Ashram,* or spiritual retreat, are now being followed by the Reverend J. C. Winslow and Dr. Stanley Jones. The use of Sanskrit for apologetic purposes is seen in the writings of Dr. John Muir and in the preaching at Benares of the late "Pundit" Johnson; and the attempt is being made to use the categories of Hinduism in the presentation of Christian thought. Now I propose in this

[1] Introduction by Dr. Fosdick to Wendell Thomas's *Hinduism Invades America.*

chapter to set forth tentatively a possible effect of the Indian environment upon the religious life of Reverend John N. Hyde.

✓The main facts of his life may be briefly stated. He was born about 1863 in Carthage, Illinois, son of a Christian minister; graduated from college and from the McCormick Theological Seminary; labored in India as a missionary from 1892 or 1893 for about twenty years, and died at his home in the United States in 1912.

At the first Sialkot Convention in 1904, he had a deep religious experience which transformed his life and influence. Before that as a missionary he had shown no special promise, but after that his life was intense. I was with him at Sialkot and on returning to Lahore heard him say in the rapture of his new experience, "Oh, I must not lose this blessing," and he never did lose it, but went on from strength to strength. During his first ten years in India, John Hyde had been very quiet and slow of speech both in English and the vernacular, but after his religious quickening at Sialkot the dumb spirit was cast out.

In the official biography he is called "Praying Hyde."[2] In and about Moga, where he lived, he was known popularly as "the man who never sleeps," a reference to his habit of long vigil at night. His prayers were of the nature of ecstatic meditation, the

[2] It consists of three parts, (I) *Praying Hyde* by Francis A. McGaw, (II) *A Vessel Unto Honour* by Rev. J. Pengwern Jones, and (III) *A Master Fisher for Souls* by Rev. R. McCheyne Paterson; the whole edited by Capt. E. G. Carré, 1930.

closest and most absorbing communion with God. In such communion he could spend hours. The Reverend Pengwern Jones mentions a day at Sialkot when from early morning till evening Mr. Hyde remained kneeling at his bedside. In answer to a request for explanation he said, "Let me tell you, what a vision I had—a new vision of Christ!" [8] It was thus an experience of meditation and communion which was productive of new spiritual insight. If the most typical religious posture of India is that of the Buddha or of some ascetic or holy man of Hinduism sitting stiffly upright, engaged in profound meditation, one can say with equal truth that the most typical religious posture of John Hyde was that of kneeling at his bedside, or lying upon his face in the "prayer room" in the agony of intercession or the rapture of communion.

The prayer room requires explanation. It began at Sialkot as the fruit of the experience of Mr. Hyde and of his conviction as to the central place of prayer. If I remember correctly, it was in the Sialkot Convention of 1905, after the preliminary Convention of 1904, that the idea of a "prayer room," as separate from a "preaching room," took root. The experience of his own deep religious quickening of the year before had filled John Hyde with a sense of the need of intercession and of the blessedness of communion.

For one or two nights at the beginning of the Convention he was alone in the place of prayer, but soon

[8] *Op. cit.*, pp. 77-79.

others joined him. John Hyde's ministry was pre eminently, in Chaucer's phrase, the ministry of "holy thought," the ministry of prayer and intercession. At the various Sialkot Conventions he could be found both day and night in the prayer room. A missionary was present at one of the Conventions who felt at first that things were not conducted properly, since the leaders and speakers were spending so much time in the prayer room. Later on, however, his eyes were opened, and with beaming face he exclaimed, "Do you know, I have found out the secret of this Convention—*it is that prayer room.* I never saw anything like it."[4] The prayer rooms—separate rooms for men and women—were arranged after the Indian fashion—no chairs, only a rug or carpet on the floor on which all could sit or kneel or lie prostrate. It was here that John Hyde got his messages, messages that thrill me yet, as I recall them, delivered in correct Hindustani with eloquence and great spiritual effectiveness, by one who before was slow of speech and anything but eloquent. I recall an Annual Meeting of the Punjab Presbyterian Mission at Ludhiana when John Hyde delivered several addresses. A senior member of the Mission who had not been slow to criticize Mr. Hyde for his queer unconventional ways was utterly astonished at the richness and helpfulness of the thoughts brought out. "Where did he get these ideas?" he exclaimed. The answer is that he got them in the secret place of prayer.

[4] *Op. cit.,* p. 76.

Obviously John Hyde's seasons of prayer might truthfully be called seasons of meditation, during which great thoughts were revealed. Prayer conceived simply as petition does not necessarily require a long time, but prayer conceived as communion with a Divine Friend may find a whole night too short. Were the ten convention days at Sialkot each year, when John Hyde hardly once slept in his bed, and also the long night vigils the rest of the year, the result of a sense of duty? In part, but far from wholly so. The seasons of prayer and holy thought were for John Hyde emotionally satisfying, for they furnished the rapture of fellowship with a Heavenly Friend. They were also intellectually quickening. Out of the prayer room at Sialkot after a night of vigil Hyde would emerge in the morning and address the people assembled in the audience room with an almost unearthly power. Once when he was suddenly called on in the morning for an address, he replied, "I haven't a single idea"; but, after receiving guidance, he went before the audience and spoke with gripping force on "The Face of the Father Bending Down in Love." In communion with the Highest he gained new visions of old truth. In this way he found those ideas which so surprised his hearers at Ludhiana.

The seasons of prayer were for John Hyde not only emotionally satisfying and intellectually quickening, but also volitionally bracing and creative. Through them he was enabled to enter more fully into the will of God for him. Through them he wrestled in the prayer room at Sialkot with "principalities and powers" and with "the world rulers of this darkness." And through the guidance received in prayer he was prompted to be as sincere and frank in the confession of personal demerit as was ever Saint Augustine or Mahatma Gandhi. So what more natural for John Hyde than to give himself to the ministry of prayer? For him prayer was indeed "the Christian's vital breath."

Naturally the place of prayer was the place for dealing with seekers. It was here that John Hyde, that "master fisher for souls," did some of his most lasting work. There was once a meeting in Wagah of the Punjab Christian Students Union. Vividly do I recall how John Hyde sat for hours on the carpet in the prayer room, surrounded by eager hearers. One of them was an Indian colleague of mine in the Forman Christian College, who hung on his words and now and then ventured a question. My impression is that he gained a great spiritual impetus on that occasion. It was the same at Sialkot. At any hour of the day or night John Hyde might be seen in the prayer room talking with the impenitent or the spiritually perplexed, or kneeling with them in prayer.

Those in spiritual need came to him. He did not have to go to them. He was sought out in the prayer room at Sialkot. He was visited at his home in Moga. Once at the Taxali Gate, Lahore, I saw an illiterate

Sadhu sitting in the cold season naked except for a loin cloth, his only warmth coming from a block of wood on fire at one end. After the day's work was over, men going home from the offices would approach the Sadhu and sit down at a respectful distance from him, getting now and then a word, and basking in the atmosphere of the Sadhu's renunciation. In somewhat the same way young men sought out John Hyde.

There was in John Hyde that utter absence of ostentation which marks the true Sadhu. One sometimes sees in India men lying on beds of spikes or swinging over fires. These things they do, "to be seen of men" and to collect alms. But the true Hindu ascetic seeks solitude, shutting the door on the outside world. The spirit of John Hyde was like that. He never mentioned in his public addresses his secret experiences of prayer. One day at Sialkot, feeling the need of being alone, he climbed into the belfry of the Hunter Memorial Church, and there in the dark poured out his soul to God. After a prolonged stay in the belfry, he descended and was immediately surrounded by a group who hung on his words. I can see him seated on the ground—a teacher in the midst of his disciples. Having finished, he arose to go his way, but was immediately surrounded by a second group. So was the man who had had fellowship with God in the secret place sought out by his fellow men.

For such holy tasks John Hyde had all the time

there was. In fact, his later ministry (1904-1912) was marked by a kind of timelessness, such as characterizes the Sadhus of India. He could talk all day to one in spiritual need, taking no account of meal time or duties. Or, if the prayer passion were upon him, he could pray all day or all night. The only other missionary, so far as I know, who had the same timeless spirit, was the late "Pundit" Johnson of Benares. Like an Indian holy man, John Hyde did not marry and so did not have to accommodate a wife in the matter of times and seasons. Even so, his queer ways must often have made him, even to those who fully understood him, something of a trial.

John Hyde was a village missionary. He early felt the need of a school for the simple training of villagers for Christian service, and at Ferozepore he set up and at first personally financed a "School of the Minor Prophets," to give the elementary training needed. This was later moved to Moga and furnished the germ out of which grew in time the Moga Training School for Village Teachers which has been of such great educational significance for the whole of India. John Hyde's prayer room in the old dispensary and the bridge under which he used to pray are still pointed out.

In his prayer life as in everything else John Hyde's supreme inspiration and example was Jesus Christ. But his long seasons of prayer and meditation, his lack of ostentation, his simple and almost ascetic ways, and the knack he had of drawing people to him by a kind of spiritual gravitation, while sufficiently accounted for by the spirit and example of his Master Christ, are nevertheless in accord with the ways of the best and most sincere Sadhus of India. Perhaps had John Hyde's ministry been in America, he would never have won the title of "Praying Hyde." Perhaps the tendency, already laid deep in his nature, toward a ministry of prayer needed, for full fruition, the influence of just such an environment as that of India, where meditation is as natural as breathing.

CHAPTER XVIII

BHANGI PRIESTHOOD, ECSTASY, AND SPIRIT-POSSESSION

THE Brahman Ramakrishna was a temple priest. At the opposite end of the social scale, the outcaste Bhangis also have priests. The Bhangis are a United Provinces group numbering some half a million. They do conservancy work in cities and are agricultural laborers in villages. Almost all are totally illiterate, but they have songs used on the great occasions of family life, birth, marriage, and death. Their songs constitute the cultural inheritance of the Bhangis. Probably, too, they have religious songs like that of the Hymn of Chet Ram. A great mass of unwritten material doubtless could be collected if the attempt were made. A Bhangi [1] is called *Lal Begi*, from Lal Beg, the patron saint of the Bhangis, *Mihtar* (prince), a mock honorific title; and he is also called sweeper, in allusion to his work.

The Bhangis may be taken as the modern representatives of the *Chandalas,* who are described by Manu [2] as born of Shudra fathers and twice-born

[1] Bhangi, probably from *bhanga* (hemp), an allusion to the drunken habits of the people.

[2] *Manusmriti,* "the Institutes of Manu," is a Hindu law-book dating from the period B.C. 200 to A.D. 200.

mothers, and so "the lowest of men," a description which "marks the Aryan abhorrence of marriage relations between women of the ruling race and men of the conquered Dravidian races." [3] A Chandala is on the same level as a pig, a cock, a dog, a menstruating woman, and a eunuch. He is called by contemptuous names, *shvapach* (dog-cooker, or possibly, one who cooks for dogs), and *apapatra* (one so unclean that his vessels must be thrown away). According to Manu, among their special tasks are carrying out the corpses of those who have no relatives and executing criminals. Dogs and donkeys (impure animals) are their wealth; their clothing, garments of the dead; their dishes for food, broken pots; their ornaments, black iron. They must live "outside the village," and "near burial grounds." They must keep to themselves.[4] Such are the disabilities under which the Chandalas of Manu's time suffered. Ethnologically, the Bhangis are clearly descended from some pre-Aryan group of aborigines, into which those have naturally gravitated, who have been expelled from their own castes. The Bhangi community, then, is a kind of Cave of Adullam, the resort of those who have no other place to go. It constitutes one of the groups which make up the fifty or sixty million "untouchables" of India. In their raw state, when uninfluenced by outside effort, their condition today is

[3] See Manu III, 239 and Crooke, E.R.E., II, 551.
[4] See *Manusmriti* X, 50-53, 55-56.

not very different from that described in the pages of Manu. While outside the pale of Hinduism in the narrow sense, they are to be reckoned, in a larger sense, as Hindus.

It was in 1921 that I found myself filling a vacancy for several months on the staff of the Saharanpur Theological Seminary, and one of my tasks was the teaching of a "village pastor's class" of young men of exceedingly limited education, most of them coming from the so-called "depressed classes." I found among them three who had been Bhangis not many years before, Hori Lal of Kasganj, Baldeo Parshad of Farrukhabad, and Bihari Lal of Etah. For about two months I questioned these, each one separately from the others, and discovered a surprisingly close agreement.

BHANGI PRIESTHOOD

The name for priest is the Vishnuite term *Bhagat* [5] (devotee). There are at least three classes of bhagats, the common bhagat who officiates for several gods and demons,[6] the bhagat who eats no meat and offers no animal sacrifices, and the *Nanakpanthi* bhagat,

[5] Sanskrit *bhakta* connected with *bhakti* "devotion."

[6] The Bhangi religion is an exuberant polytheism which includes a large number of village gods, godlings and demons, Kankali, Bhairon, Bhawani, Masan, Khais, Churail, Tarajogini, Halaka, Bundela, Chamardevi, Gamadevi, Nagarsen, Ahut, Jakhaiya, etc., etc. Along with these, which may be called as it were, *outcaste gods,* there is also, theoretically at least, the worship of the classic gods of Hinduism.

who represents the Udasi ascetic order of heretical Sikhism.[7]

There are two methods of becoming a bhagat. The first is by imitation. A man carefully watches the procedure of worship and is able to copy it without special instruction. Baldeo Parshad is an illustration of this method, for he conducted the worship of Nagarsen for a year or more. His desire to become a Bhangi bhagat was, as he put it, in order that by means of ecstasy he might arouse the wonder of the people. But the inspiration to pass into ecstasy (a mental state hypnotic in character) never came. The second method of becoming a bhagat—the ordinary method—is by instruction. A man learns the work from an experienced priest, a year or more being required for the purpose. The priesthood among the Bhangis is usually hereditary, in the sense that a son learns the work from his father, if he is a bhagat. Bihari Lal mentioned a family in which four generations had furnished a bhagat. The office of a priest may be dropped at any time, hence it is mostly occasional, not regular.

In order to be trained as a priest a young man goes to a bhagat and asks to become a disciple. He replies: "Very well; you must worship the gods." So

[7] The Udasi order of Sikh ascetics has carried on considerable missionary work among the depressed classes. Those won to Sikhism are called *Mazhabi*, that is, "religious" Sikhs, Sikhs by religion not by race. Once in Fatehgarh, U. P., I heard of a bhagat who had great influence over the Bhangis there. On looking him up, I found that he was a Nanakpanthi bhagat.

the bhagat explains the ritual of worship. Then he leads his new disciple to the Ganges, or to another stream if the Ganges be far away, taking along at the same time the leaves of the betel nut. Both bhagat and novice enter the river up to the middle. The bhagat asks, "Will you serve Chamardevi?" On the answer "Yes," the bhagat puts the leaf of the betel nut into the mouth of the candidate and immerses him completely. The same question—and here is the polytheistic element—is asked concerning each divinity in turn, Kali (whom Ramakrishna regarded as his "mother"), Jwaladevi, and the others. "Will you serve so-and-so?" and in each case the betel-leaf is placed in the mouth of the novice and he is totally immersed.

Now the scene shifts from the river to the house of the novice, where the bhagat conducts a "high service." Both the novice and his wife receive from the bhagat the laying on of hands and they bow down to the ground at the name of each god. Now the bhagat makes two knotted strings to go round both their necks as amulets, and instructs them to sacrifice to the gods every Monday. There is a difference between the "high service" and the "low service," which consists in the presence or absence of animal sacrifices. The novice and his wife are commanded not to eat any unclean thing, such as carrion and beef, nor to enter the home of a lying-in woman during the ten days of her impurity. Otherwise, the knotted strings around their necks will become impure, and they will be defiled.

For a year the candidate performs "low service" every Monday. At the end of the year the bhagat receives from his disciple the usual tutorial fee—a full suit of clothes (five pieces), one turban, one bottle of country liquor, and five rupees. So the novice becomes a full-fledged bhagat. The Bhangis have nothing of the nature of a school for the preparation of priests. The relation of a bhagat to a disciple is personal, reminding one of former days in America, when a student of theology often read under the direction of some minister. The majority of Bhangi bhagats are quite illiterate.

There are recognized signs of fitness for becoming a bhagat. Such are cleanliness, not eating the food left over by others, singing the songs of the gods, and pleasure in seeing the worship of the gods, and very specially the ability to fall into a state of ecstasy.[8] Bihari Lal mentioned a lad who had the above-mentioned qualities, and later became a bhagat. He was highly regarded by his community. It looks as if to become a bhagat was for him the very best thing he knew, and a sign of religious earnestness. *Khelna* (playing) seems to be infectious, for Bihari Lal said that once when, as a small boy, he was watching a bhagat "play," he himself began also to "play." At

[8] The technical term for this in Hindustani is *khelna,* lit. "to play." When one falls into this highly emotional state, quivering violently, and grunting (a kind of Bhangi "speaking with tongues"), one is said "to play."

Saharanpur he showed, for my information, how "playing" is done.

A certain amount of fasting is part of a bhagat's life. When *puja* (worship) takes place, he always fasts until the *puja* is completed. Saturday, Sunday and Monday, are special days for worship. The bhagat's dress is peculiar. He has long hair, a string of *rudraksha* beads about his neck, an amulet, naked feet, a *tika* (religious mark) on his forehead, the dress of an ascetic, etc.

Hori Lal of Kasganj had a cousin who became a bhagat, although at the time he was known as a Christian. One day he began to "play," shaking his head and quivering. His father and Hori Lal's father gave him a good beating, and so he desisted.

There are also women bhagats who worship especially godlings and demons. Theirs are the more insignificant kinds of worship, such as the pouring out of water as a drink offering in honor of some goddess, or the giving of a religious song or dance. When a group of women go to a *than* (shrine) for worship, the most venerable woman among them will officiate as priestess, offering the gifts on the shrine, while the rest of the women play musical instruments and sing.

There are two forms of the altar at which the Bhangi priest officiates, the *than*[9] and the *chauk*. The *than* is an earthen or brick structure elevated a

[9] *Than*, from Skt., *sthana* (place), hence sacred place.

foot or more above the ground. It consists of a level platform, and at one end the structure is built up from one to three feet above the level of the platform, and contains one or more niches to hold lights. The niches usually face the rising sun (the eastward position). In front of the upright position of the *than,* there are frequently to be found five little pinnacles, four set in a square and one in the middle of the square. Each Bhangi quarter in a village has, as a rule, one *than.* Some one belonging to that quarter is usually trained as a bhagat, so as to officiate as priest. Bihari Lal described how forty Bhangis united in erecting a shrine. Worship at such a Bhangi shrine consists in lighting each evening a wick and placing it in the niche on the *than,* this being the task of the local bhagat or of some one appointed by him.

The *chauk* [10] is a small square about three by two feet, plastered over with cow-dung (as a sacred substance), and then ornamented with lines and circles in white. In the sacred square are placed the things which belong to Bhangi worship, a live coal (*agyari*), sacred flowers, especially marigold, cloves, red lead, a preparation of opium, rice, sweets and a bottle of country liquor. The celebrant sits on the ground, cross-legged, before the door of the *chauk.* During worship melted butter is dropped on the live coal, and flares up. Such a *chauk,* or "sacred square," may

[10] *Chauk,* from Skt., *chatushka* (four-sided).

be prepared in a room, a courtyard, or out in the field.

At a "high service" the bhagat officiates at the shrine. In addition to grain and sweets, the people bring a cock and a young pig, which are decapitated. The first drops of blood are sprinkled on the live coal as a fire-altar. The flesh is cooked and with bread constitutes a *parshad,* or sacramental meal, of which all, men, women and children, partake. The belief is that participation in the holy meal protects one from ghosts and demons.

Chamardevi is worshipped every Monday by those who own water buffaloes, a bit of buffalo-ghee being offered. The goddess is represented by a rude stone or by an engraved stone from some old temple. The stone is anointed with the melted butter and the worshipper bows down to the ground, saying, "I worship thy feet; do thou protect me and my children and my cattle, and all my neighbors." We may compare the story of Jacob at Bethel.

The "high service" of Chamardevi is more elaborate, the ceremony being performed by a regular bhagat, on behalf of a sick person. The animal sacrifice consists of a male lamb of one year, unblemished, of one color, black or white, but not of mixed color. Before the lamb is killed he is waved around and over the head of the sick from three to twenty-one times. This is the "wave" ceremony. Now the bhagat lays his hand upon the head of the victim, saying: "Goddess, here is your lamb. Now be satisfied. Let protection be over us all." This is the prayer of dedication and the laying of hands on the head of the victim. The bhagat severs the head of the lamb with one blow of a large knife, and the head is placed in front of the stone that represents Chamardevi. Automatically the mouth opens a few times before life is extinct. The people think that the slaughtered lamb is uttering a word. Some blood falls upon the fire as the head is severed. From the ashes of the *agyari*, or "sacred fire," a *tika* is applied to the forehead of the sick man, and the bhagat makes a knotted string for his neck. This account was derived from Bihari Lal of Etah. Baldeo Parshad of Farrukhabad had never seen the worship of Chamardevi.

When small-pox appears, people say, "*Sitaladevi* has come"; when it becomes worse, they say: "The goddess is angry." The bhagat makes an arrangement, telling the kind of gift that will appease the goddess. Thus one of the bhagat's functions is that of a medicine-man or healer. When one is sick of the small-pox, fresh water is drawn from the well and poured out as a drink offering to the Devi. When a cow gives only half as much milk as expected, she is regarded as affected by a demon. So they have recourse to a bhagat. When a cow has given a calf, the first milk is offered to *Gamadevi;* if there is no *than,* then in the name of the Devi it is poured out on the ground.

BHANGI ECSTASY

When a novice has finished his novitiate, his *guru* is called to perform a "high service." Five or ten live coals are placed on a "sacred square," one for each god. The preceptor bhagat soon begins to "play." Shaking and quivering he says to his disciple, "You are my horse." The people think that the bhagat is possessed by some devi. As the bhagat continues to shake his head in the orgy of possession, he says to his disciple: "Give me my perquisites." So he formally receives the customary fee. Bihari Lal declared that the whole business of *khelna* is for the sake of a livelihood. He admitted, however, that bhagats, as a rule, regard their ecstatic experiences as real.

A woman, when officiating as a priestess for a group of women, will often begin to "play." It being assumed that she is "possessed" by some spirit or demon, the usual questions are asked of her, for example, "Who are you? Are you pleased with the worship?" If any one is ill, enquiry is made of the goddess Gamadevi, who is supposed to have taken possession of the priestess; also, if anything of value has been lost. Thus the officiating priestess acts as a medium, ecstatic, soothsayer, and witch-doctor. While she really does the work of a priestess, she is not publicly recognized as such. Baldeo Parshad's mother and aunt have both officiated as priestesses.

Not only men and women "play," but also children. Bihari Lal reported that from the age of seven to fourteen he often "played." Did this have anything to do with his rather unsatisfactory state of health? One may compare Ramakrishna's experiences of ecstasy and trance, when a child.

In the all-night worship of *Jwaladevi* several bhagats officiate. When the chief bhagat begins to "play," he at first shakes his clasped hands gently, then more violently, so that the bells fastened to his waist rattle. The special bhagat and the two or more acolytes dance all night to the music and song of the choir behind. This is the dancing form of ecstasy, well known throughout the Himalayas.

Ahut means the spirit of a dead uncle, which receives offerings once or twice a year. The cooked food offered is regarded as holy, and to eat it is a sign of humility. In connection with a "high service" for an *ahut,* a young pig is sacrificed, and the celebrant not only "plays" violently, but also weeps. Meditation on the *ahut* is regarded as meritorious on the part of relatives.

In the ecstatic "play" the following activities are to be distinguished: opening the mouth and taking breath; rocking back and forth gently for a minute or two; violent shaking of the head, first in a sitting position and then with the two hands propped on the ground; uttering the syllable *hu* or *hun;* sometimes dancing.

The phenomena of ecstasy are widespread throughout the world and date from remote antiquity.[11]

BHANGI SPIRIT-POSSESSION AND EXORCISM

Ecstasy is almost always taken as a sign of possession. The ecstatic is asked, "Who are you?" and the answer is: "I am Chamardevi" or "Gamadevi," or the spirit of some dead person, or some demon or other. A woman complained that a *bhut* (demon) was troubling her. A bhagat was called and soon began to "play." In answer to the question, "Who are you?" he replied, "I am Chamardevi." Then the husband of the woman supposed to be possessed asked: "Mother, these demons that are in my wife, whence have they come?" The bhagat (by implication, Chamardevi) replied, "You have not worshipped me; therefore I have sent the demons." The request followed, "Mother Chamardevi, receive worship and seize the demons." The goddess speaking through the bhagat replies: "I will seize one demon; Kalidevi, another; Kalkadevi, a third; Nathiyadevi, a fourth; and Karedeo, a fifth." For the business of exorcism there were three bhagats present, and they prepared to seize the demons by the aid of the gods

11 A reference to the very important article in E.R.E. on *Priest: Priesthood (Primitive)* by G. Landtman makes it clear that the Bhangi priesthood is as archaic as anything of the sort on earth. We may compare the infectious character of the bhagat's "play" with a similar situation as described in 1 Samuel XIX, 18-24. See also for China, *Demon Possession and Allied Themes* by Dr. Nevius.

and goddesses. As usual, a *chauk* is prepared with an *agyari*. The woman supposed to be possessed by a demon is set close to the *agyari,* "sacred fire," with the three bhagats, one on each side of her and one behind. A song is sung, and soon the woman begins to "play," that is, the *bhut* has come. The bhagats ask, "Who art thou?" The woman (that is the *bhut* speaking through the woman) replies: "I am the head man of village so and so [a dead man]. This woman goes past my shrine and does not offer me obeisance." The three bhagats then cry out: "Chamardevi, seize the demon." The bhagats proceed to make knots in the woman's hair, so that the indwelling demon may not escape by way of the hair. The *bhut* finally says, "Let me go; I will never come back." The *bhut* is permitted to leave on taking an oath to this effect. The people present were fully convinced that the *bhut* had been caught and expelled by Chamardevi. Hori Lal was a witness of this exorcism.

Just as Chamardevi caught one demon, so each *devi* catches a demon. When all the demons which have entered a man or woman have been caught, then a "high service" takes place. In catching the demons a strand of hair of the one possessed is tied, in the name of each god or goddess. When the demons are all cast out, then the strands of hair that are tied are cut and burned in the fire. The work of exorcism being completed, the bhagats go their way. Such is the exorcism of a common demon.

A leper and a woman during the period of her

ceremonial impurity are loathsome objects, to be avoided. Hence the spirit of a dead leper is a leprous demon, and the spirit of a woman who has died within ten days after child-bearing is a filthy *churail*. Both demons are exceedingly hard to cast out. A filthy *churail* frequents trees, dark and filthy places, and pools. Her feet turn backward; her mouth is twisted; and her teeth are very large and projecting. Her breasts are exposed, and her mouth is wide open. As usual bhagats are called, in order to expel her. In an earthen vessel are placed certain things which women love, such as red lead, bangles, rings, red cloth, combs, looking glasses, sweets, etc., in order to tempt the female demon to come out of the one possessed and enter the vessel. Then the cover is clapped on tight and pressed down, so as to imprison the demon. The vessel is then carried to crossroads, where it is left.

Hori Lal told the following story. His uncle's wife was possessed by a *churail,* as she and others believed. All of her children died in infancy except one son. When he was ill at the age of two, he would shake his head, twist his face horribly, and foam at the mouth. When Hori Lal's aunt "played," she (that is, the *churail* in her) would say: "This is my sister. I will never leave her." The *churail* was identified as the ghost of a younger sister. The evil deeds of a *churail,* according to popular belief, are the following: kills young children; kills mother and infant at childbirth; goes with a bride to her husband's home and takes possession of her; seduces young men through dreams.

To sum up, Bhangi religion is a religion of fear, consisting largely in the propitiation or magic control of malevolent ghosts and demons. Ecstasy is greatly prized as the prophetic afflatus *par excellence,* which opens the door into a world of spirit-possession and supernatural activities. Syncretism holds sway, the cult of village gods and demons of aboriginal and Dravidian origin being combined, at least nominally, with that of the great Aryan gods. The Vedic god *Jam* (Skt. *Yama,* "the King of the dead") is recognized, when death draws near. The *havan* ceremony through the dropping of "melted butter" into the fire, and the waving of lights, the *arati* ceremony, are also observed, both being very early Aryan practices. Bloody sacrifices are common, especially of the pig and the chicken, and the sprinkling of blood on the fire altar. Sacred places are the *than* and the *chauk,* together with the sacred rivers, etc., of Hinduism. There is the sacramental use of bathing, and a sacramental meal of bread and flesh. Stones which represent gods are anointed with oil. The priestly bhagat conducts worship, trains novitiates for the office of the priesthood, acts as medicine-man or healer in cases of illness, in the ecstatic state is a diviner, or soothsayer, for the finding of lost things, and casts out evil spirits, such as the leprous demon and the *churail.* The Bhangi "death-feast" includes the service and worship of the dead.

The belief in spirit-possession is of immemorial antiquity. There is a clear reference to it in Rigveda X, 136, where the Vedic *Munis* are described as being like the ascetics and bhagats of modern times, in having long hair, wearing yellow garments, drinking draughts that produce ecstasy, and in being taken possession of by the gods. Popular Hinduism in general, as well as Bhangi religion in particular, are everywhere marked by belief in demon-possession and the practice of demon exorcism.

CHAPTER XIX

THE CHUHRAS, AN ETHNOLOGICAL PROBLEM

THE Chuhras are a depressed community found in the northern and western Punjab.[1]

The term "Hindu Chuhras" covers by a process of elimination all who have not become Sikhs, Musalmans or Christians. They are called "Hindus" only by courtesy. The Census of India report for 1921 contains the following statement: "They are looked down on by their Hindu neighbors. No Brahman ministers to them. They are not allowed to enter Hindu places of worship, and they are supposed to cause contamination by touch." The next decade, however (1921-1931), witnessed distinct progress in the amelioration of the untouchables. The reformed Hindu societies[2] are all doing more or less for the outcastes. Notable is the work of the Depressed Classes Mission Society of India with its center at Bombay. Christian Missions were early in this field

1 Chuhra numbers according to the

	1901	1911	1921
Census of India	1,329,418	1,269,250	1,190,334
Hindu Chuhras		789,915	708,680
Musalman Chuhras		393,718	374,945
Sikh Chuhras		73,100	106,709

2 Arya Samaj, Deva Samaj, Brahmo Samaj, Prarthana Samaj, Radha Soami Satsang, Ramakrishna Mission, etc.

and continue to work diligently. As the result of the enlightened policy of the Maharaja of Baroda in furnishing a scholarship for study in the West, Bhim Rao Ramji Ambedkar, a Mahar "untouchable" received the degree of Ph.D. at Columbia University, and was a member of both Round Table Conferences in London. Specially significant are the strong utterances against untouchability on the part of such men as the Hon. G. K. Gokhale, Lala Lajpat Rai, and Mahatma Gandhi.

In 1921 Islam had some 375,000 members of Chuhra origin, called *musallis* (prayerful), or *dindar* (devout). The Chuhras of the Rawalpindi District and of the North West Frontier Province have almost entirely embraced Islam.

In the same year Sikhism had 107,000 *mazhabi* or "religious" Sikhs, Sikhs by religion, not by race, an increase of some 33,000 over 1911. The Udasi order of ascetics is a great propaganda society. "Though good Sikhs so far as religious observance is concerned, the taint of hereditary pollution is upon them" (that is upon converts from the Chuhras); "and Sikhs of other castes refuse to associate with them even in religious ceremonies."[8] We may compare the religious separateness from other Christians of the Negroes of America.

Christianity in the Punjab is drawing large numbers from the Chuhras. Probably the loss of about 100,000 Chuhras (1911-1921) by Hinduism and Islam

[8] Ibbetson, *Census of India, 1881*, reprint as *Panjab Castes*, 1916.

is due largely to the gains of the Christian Church.[4]

The Chuhras are chameleon-like in their copying of the externals of other faiths. Those serving Moslem landlords gradually adopt Moslem customs; those serving Sikh landlords, Sikh customs; while those who become Christians are frequently content with a thin veneer of Christianity on top of their previous religious practices. This religious flexibility, or ease of adjustment to environment, has made the Chuhras "the chief disturbing element in the return of religions in the Punjab." [5]

As regards occupation and social status, the condition of the Chuhras of the Punjab is practically identical with that of the Bhangis of the United Provinces. The city-dwelling Chuhras as a rule do scavenging work. Hence, like the Bhangis, they are called "sweepers." [6] They live in the slums of cities and physically show the effect of their environment. The village Chuhras, as regards work, pay, and living quarters, are very much like the village Bhangis. There are, however, two points of difference. The Bhangi rears pigs, the scavenger animals of India; the Chuhra, as a rule, does not. And, as compared with the Bhangi, the Chuhra is usually tall and powerful.

In cities, Christians of Chuhra origin are very frequently house servants. We had a Chuhra Christian

[4] The supreme social service of Christian Missions in India has been the inauguration of work among the outcastes.

[5] *Census of India, 1921*, XV, Pt. I, 178.

[6] The name *Chuhra* may possibly be derived from the Hindi *Chuhra Pharna* (to sweep up *rubbish*) (Crooke).

cook by the name of Tuni, the best cook we ever had and exceptionally neat and clean. A non-Christian sweeper, Chuhra or Bhangi, it is uncertain which, once served us, whose utter faithfulness in his work still remains with us as a grateful memory.

The Chuhras are divided into *gots,*[7] many of which, with their numbers, are mentioned in the Census of 1881. Such are, for example, Sahotra (79,551), Gil (77,613), Untwal (18,781), etc. The *got* name is very like a family name in the West. One has but to glance into a published genealogy of a large family, where a single ancestor may have thousands of descendants, to observe the resemblance. Each *got,* as a rule, has its own peculiar religious customs, such as a clearly recognized tabu, and special ceremonies of ancestor worship. The object which is *tabu,* that is, must not be killed, used or abused, is usually an animal or plant, but may be almost any object. Toward such a sacred object there is a "superstitious awe" on the part of the clan.[8] The tiger (wild cat, or leopard) is sacred to one clan, the rabbit to another; and in like manner, wolf, fish, cloves, egg-plant, burnt brick, branches of particular trees, and many other things, are inviolable objects to particularly Chuhra clans. This system of tabus strongly resembles totemism. A Chuhra Christian, whose wife had belonged to a tiger-reverencing clan, took

[7] *Got,* Skt. *gotra* (clan).

[8] See *The Religion and Customs of the Chuhra in the Panjab Province, India,* by H. J. Strickler, 1926 (in manuscript).

her to the zoo. When she saw a leopard, she covered her face and did obeisance.

The great festivals of Hinduism, such as Holi and Diwali, are occasions for a kind of ancestor worship within each clan. Melted butter is poured, drop by drop, upon the sacred fire, and at each drop the name of a dead ancestor or other relative is mentioned. In this way, the *Kuldeo,*[9] or "family god," possibly to be identified with the most important ancestor, is recognized. This may, however, be little more than a method of grateful remembrance, like the use of flowers on Decoration Day in America.

The Chuhras worship Bala Shah (= Lal Beg, Balmik).[10] Their shrines, like those of the Bhangis, are called *than.* The shrines of Chuhras who work for Muhammadans frequently resemble Muhammadan shrines, and worship at a Chuhra shrine in the western Punjab is usually on Thursday evening corresponding to the time of Muhammadan worship. When all the Chuhras of a place become Christians, then with some fear and trembling the shrine is destroyed. The Chuhra *than* is sometimes substantially made of burnt brick, and there are well-built Chuhra temples at Nakodar and Ferozepore in the Punjab.

In their fear of ghosts and evil spirits the Chuhras

9 "They (Chuhras) are said also to have family gods (*Kuldeo*) whose names they never divulge, and to whom offerings are made on holidays, and at births and deaths in the family"—Crooke, *Bhangi,* in E.R.E.

10 Balmik (Skt. *Valmiki*) the poet sage, who compiled the Epic of the Ramayana. In some inexplicable way Lal Beg has been mixed up with the cult of Valmiki. Crooke, *Bhangi,* in E.R.E.

are like the Bhangis. Bad dreams are due to the pressure, and sickness to the shadow, of evil spirits, and almost every untoward event is referred to the same cause. Thus there is a very large assortment of demons. Naturally, then, much of the Chuhra religion consists in the pacifying of diabolic powers through sacrifice and gifts. While largely a religion of fear, it is not wholly so. Good spirits are also recognized. They bring blessing. They attach themselves to wood [11] and to other things, especially cooking vessels.

Priests are called *Pir*. They do duty at marriages and funerals. Sadhus or *faqirs* are of five kinds, each kind differing from the others in dress, etc. Their work is to expel evil spirits by means of their incantations.

Three layers of religious belief and practice may possibly be distinguished among the Chuhras: (1) the rites of a gotra, or clan, including its special tabu and special ancestral worship; (2) the special tribal religion with its worship of Bala Shah; and (3) a thin veneer of belief or practice due to association as workmen with Hindus, Moslems, Sikhs, or Christians.

The late Dr. Youngson discovered in the Sialkot district the manuscript of an extensive series of poems [12] relating to the religious and social life of the Chuhras. The manuscript is written in Muhamma-

[11] Compare "Touch wood."

[12] Published in the *Indian Antiquary*, Vols. XXXV-XXXVI (1906-1907).

dan Punjabi, in which the script is Persian and the vocabulary largely so. The discovery is important for the study of the Chuhra wedding and other family customs. It is also a rich source for the religious ideas of the Chuhras, such as the attributes of God, the nature of Bala Shah, prayer, legendary lore, traditions as to the creation, dedication of a shrine, etc. The following articles of Chuhra faith were extracted from it by Dr. Youngson: [13] One God; one High Priest Bala Shah, who is also a Mediator,[14] to whom they pray. Sin is a reality. Sacrifice is part of the worship of God. The spirit of a man at death returns to God, and there will be a resurrection [15] of the body, a day of judgment; heaven and hell.

The articles of faith mentioned above represent the Islamic belief in one God, and resurrection from the dead as superimposed upon the substructure of the Chuhra doctrine of Bala Shah. It illustrates the Indian practice of religious syncretism. There is no clear reference to Christian beliefs, except as mediated through Islam. Bala Shah is described as a representative or incarnation of God.[16]

[13] See *Ind. Ant.*, XXXV, 354 and especially Art. *Chuhra* in E.R.E.

[14] "Our cry is to thee; thy cry reaches the presence of God."

[15] Compare the following Chuhra hymn (as translated):

"But see, the house is darkened, the soul has taken flight
To God, who takes account of the deeds of sense and sight;
Alone, a homeless wanderer, she now is doomed to roam,
But at the resurrection the Lord will bring her home."

[16] Dr. Youngson (E.R.E. III, 616) mentions Ibbetson's remark that the religion of the Chuhras is nearer Christianity in its principles than any other Indian religion.

The Chuhra poems are committed to memory, representing as they do the traditional lore and culture of the community.[17]

In Lahore I once witnesed a Chuhra *jag*[18] (high service) at a Balmiki shrine. It was in the evening and about fifty people were present; men, children and a few women. The *halwa,* or cooked sweetbread, an offering to Balmik, was placed on the *thara,* or level platform of the shrine, and then the lights were lighted. The singing[19] began, accompanied by a drum and harmonium. It was very good, two sometimes singing together, but never the whole company. During the singing incense was burned. A dog tried to steal the sweetbread. He was driven off, and the people shouted: *Bolo, mo'mino Wuhi Ek* (Say, believers, He is one). A fire of coals was now set on the platform beneath the lights. In front of the fire was the platter of sweetbread, some of which was taken and in the form of five balls placed around the fire. Melted butter was poured on the fire, and the fire-waving ceremony ensued. Next two men stood side by side on the platform of the shrine facing the lights, each holding on the palms of his hands a small platter containing a lighted wick. One of them re-

17 Compare Nathaniel Schmidt's *Coming Religion,* 1930, p. 165: "Through long periods of human history practically all education consisted in the transmission within the clan and the tribe of sacred traditions." Quoted by permission of the Macmillan Company, publishers.

18 Hindi *jag* = Skt. *Yajna* (sacrifice, or high service).

19 The tunes were in general the same indigenous tunes as are set to the Punjabi metrical translations of the Psalms prepared by the Punjab United Presbyterian Mission.

cited a long litany, all of the people standing at this supreme moment. Next prayer was offered, ending with the shout on the part of all, *Sri Balmik ki jai* (Victory to Balmik). A collection was taken to pay the musicians. The final ceremony was the distribution of the sweetbread to all present—men, women and children, each receiving a ball of it, to be eaten as a kind of communion with Balmik and with one another. Participation in the *parshad,* or sacramental feast, at a high service is the method of initiating outsiders into the Chuhra community.

The whole ritual lasted one and one-half hours. The two celebrants were Chuhra head men. The service was fixed and formal from beginning to end, the ritualistic elements consisting of lights on the shrine, incense, singing, prayer, the *arati* ceremony of the waving of lights, the chanting of a litany, *havan,* or the pouring of ghee into the fire (an ancient Vedic rite), participation in a sacramental feast; a collection of money, and the united shouting of sacred formulas. At the time of the litany and prayer the service was distinctly impressive. On the whole, it was very orderly and reverent.

The question remains, who are the Chuhras? Some think they are of pre-Aryan, or Dravidian origin. There is a general tendency to regard the outcastes and "untouchables" as aborigines.[20] The aboriginal and mixed origin of the Bhangis scarcely admits of doubt, and the Chuhras certainly resemble

[20] See Ibbetson, *Punjab Castes,* pp. 266-267, 293.

the Bhangis in occupation, religion, and social status. The view that the average Chuhra is somewhat darker than the Brahman or Sikh, may, if true, point in the same direction.[21] The Chuhra tabus, also, which look like the relics of Totemism, resemble similar customs found especially in the population of central and southern India. One can also discover here and there vague traditions that originally all the land belonged to the Chuhras, but that when the present Hindus came, the Chuhras were reduced to serfdom.[22]

There is however another view represented by excellent scholars, that the Chuhras are of Aryan origin. According to Risley [23] the scavenging Chuhra of the Punjab "is cast in much the same mould as the Rajput of Udaipur and Marwar." In other words, as specimens of the Indo-Aryan type, Risley selects, on the basis of anthropometry, the Rajput and the Chuhra. Risley is followed by the *Imperial Gazetteer* of India and the *Cambridge Ancient History of India.*

Consider the clan name "Gil." There are Hindu, Musalman, and Sikh as well as Chuhra Gil. I once heard a Sikh sardar of Moga explain that the various

21 Compare the proverb quoted by H. J. Strickler in his M.A. Dissertation: "A dark Brahman, a fair Chuhra, a woman with a beard, these are contrary to nature."

22 The theory of an ancient dignity may, however, be only a compensatory reaction against the present "inferiority complex" which characterizes the Chuhra community. See also H. J. Strickler, *op. cit.*, Chap. I.

23 *People of India*, Ed. Crooke, 1915, pp. 37, 43, 358-359.

Gil were originally all of one stock, some remaining Hindus, others becoming Musalmans or Sikhs, and still others for some reason becoming "depressed," as the Chuhra Gil. Ibbetson gives another explanation of this: [24] "It seems to me more than probable that in old days, when menials were bound more closely to the tribes they served, the names of these tribes were used to distinguish the several groups of menials." Baines [25] ventures a further suggestion: If the Chuhras (viewed as Aryan) entered India very early, they may have been overwhelmed "by subsequent invaders and reduced to servitude." Their present habitat in the northern and western Punjab might, however, seem to indicate that they entered India from the northwest comparatively late, perhaps during the early Christian centuries.

The evidence of anthropometry, and especially of craniometry, is disputed by some anthropologists.[26] It is clear that much more research is necessary. We must end, then, as we began, leaving the Chuhras "an ethnological problem."

[24] *Punjab Castes*, p. 20.
[25] *Ethnology*, p. 78.
[26] Especially by Professor Franz Boas of Columbia University.

CHAPTER XX

COMMINGLING OF HINDU AND MUSLIM WORSHIP AT POPULAR SHRINES

IN THE city of Lahore there is the shrine of a well-known Muslim saint, *Data Ganj-Bakhsh* (Liberal Treasure-giver), who belonged to the period of the earliest Muhammadan occupation of Lahore. Once I visited the shrine in company with a Muslim student of the Forman Christian College. We removed our shoes at the entrance and walked about in our stocking feet, going everywhere with perfect liberty. The thing which especially impressed me was that not only Muslims were doing obeisance at the shrine, but also Hindus and Sikhs. The saint was "the giver of treasure," and I listened with deep interest to Hindu and Sikh women who made known their requests at the Muhammadan shrine, one, a barren woman, asking for a child, another presenting the case of a sick relative, and so on. I was vividly reminded of Chaucer's account of the mediæval cavalcade journeying to the tomb of St. Thomas à Becket, at Canterbury,

> The holy blissful martyr for to seeke,
> That hem hath holpen when that they were seeke.

Such common reverence for a holy man on the part of both Hindus and Muhammadans is no new thing in India, for in the fifteenth century "Kabir, the weaver saint, was claimed by both Muslims and Hindus."[1]

On another occasion I was present at a series of religious lectures given at Jalesar in the Etah District. Jalesar is an ancient site marked by a very large mound, which rises fifty or more feet above the plain. No one knows the ancient name, unless it was Jaleshwara. During one of the days of our stay we noticed a constant stream of people wending their way toward a shrine up in the fields. The story of the saint there worshipped, as I recall it, struck us as strange and even weird. But most interesting to us was the fact that both Muslims and Hindus joined in the weekly worship at the shrine, and that our host, a Muhammadan gentleman of the place, had a proprietary right to a portion of the gifts brought by devotees. I think we "chaffed" him a bit on his participation in such worship.

Another example, not so much of united worship at a popular shrine as of a Hindu sect with a Muhammadan head, may be cited. There is in the Punjab (or was some years ago) a group of Hindu goldsmiths and silversmiths known as *Shamsis,* whose supreme teacher and head is the well-known Muslim grandee, the *Aga Khan.* Him they regard as in some

[1] See Art. *Religion in Contemporary India* by Nicol Macnicol, *Hibbert Journal,* Oct. 1931, p. 41.

sense an expression of God. Once when the Aga Khan was in Lahore, a group of his Hindu disciples came to meet him. I looked them up. I found them somewhat disappointed, as they had not caught even a glimpse of their preceptor. But they declared their strong faith in him. The Shamsis are a semi-secret religious sect.

What is the significance of these facts? The great problem of India's future is the Hindu-Muslim problem, the question whether these two major communities will live in peace and work together for the good of India. But why should they not? The vast majority of the seventy million Muslims of India are descended from Hindu ancestors and are not foreigners but genuine Indians. And in the matter of religion there is a vast common ground consisting in the worship of the sainted dead, *pir, paighambar, sant, sadhu,* in which people of both communities often join. And even in the metaphysical doctrine of God there are points of contact. The Muslim confession of faith, "There is no god but God," is paralleled by the rigid monism of the great Upanishad utterance, "One only without a second." Both confessions (of course with differences) deny the possibility of any "companion" to God. Then there are the pantheistic resemblances between the Sufiism of Islam and the Vedanta of Hinduism.[2] It is, of course, not to be expected, nor would it be desirable, that Hindus

[2] See *Indian Islam* by Murray T. Titus, 1930, p. 110, and *Indian Social Reformer,* Nov. 7, 1931, p. 147.

and Muslims should seek a least common denominator of their faiths. But all men of good will who believe in God, however defined, in an "unseen universe," and in the supreme importance of the ethical should live together in mutual respect, and may well join hands against irreligion and in defense of a spiritual interpretation of the universe.

Thus the links connecting the Hindu and Muslim communities are impressive–common habitat, common speech, generally common blood, common elements of popular faith, and even some points of likeness in their metaphysical positions, as well as a common interest in the welfare of India.

CHAPTER XXI

HAR DAYAL AND N. SEN GUPTA, INDIAN REVOLUTIONARIES

HAR DAYAL [1] was a graduate student of the Government College, Lahore, in 1903-1904, having taken his B.A. degree from St. Stephen's College, Delhi. He attended my lectures on Tennyson's *In Memoriam* in the Forman Christian College, Lahore, an arrangement existing between these two Lahore colleges of the Punjab University for joint lectures in M.A. English subjects. Along with his fellow students he sought to master the text of *In Memoriam*, and at the same time, as a work of supererogation, he committed a large part of the poem to memory. One evening he gave a public exhibition of his powers of memory. Eight or ten masses of strange, unconnected material, including several long sentences in Pushtu, were successively sounded into his ears for him to assimiliate and reproduce. Everything came out in the order in which it went in, and perfectly. It was an example in modern India of the high development in ancient India of the same faculty, by which, for example, the whole text of the Rigveda

1 This account of Har Dayal's activities is based on Sir Michael O'Dwyer's *India as I Knew It, 1885-1925*, together with the personal recollections of my wife and myself.

could be carried in the memory of those who were in a very real sense "living manuscripts." One may wonder whether such a high development of memory may not at times co-exist with a defective judgment. On the other hand, it must be admitted that a highly developed memory makes possible, even in illiterate ages and illiterate communities, the acquisition of great masses of cultural material, poems, stories, etc., which would otherwise be largely impossible.

Har Dayal acquitted himself so brilliantly in the examination for the M.A. degree that he received a Government of India scholarship for several years of study in England, where he was enrolled in 1905 as a student in St. John's College, Oxford. What happened there is unknown to me beyond the fact that he became embittered and in 1907 threw down his scholarship. He returned to India in profound disillusionment, and, in the words of Sir Michael O'Dwyer, "thenceforward devoted his undoubted talents to revolutionary work." Forced to leave India before long, he took refuge in California early in 1911 where for several years he worked up the *ghadr* (mutiny) movement among the Hindu and Sikh immigrants, all the time keeping in close touch with India and inspiring the revolutionary activities there.

In 1914 the United States Government, owing to representations from Great Britain, arrested Har Dayal with a view to deportation as an undesirable alien. He was released on bail, but he forfeited his bail and fled to Switzerland. During the Great War he was in Germany, most of the time in Berlin. At the close of the War letters of his published in one of the Indian papers would seem to indicate that he had to some extent suffered a change of heart. He has for obvious reasons never returned to India. At last accounts he was in Sweden teaching Sanskrit in one of the Universities and giving lectures on India throughout the country.

The incident, in May 1913, of the bomb in the Government Gardens, Lahore, throws a vivid light on the revolutionary activities of Har Dayal. One evening between eight and nine o'clock we heard a loud report. It was thought at first that it was the nine o'clock gun. It proved to be a bomb, which had been picked up by an Indian messenger on the road close to the Lahore Club and had exploded, killing him. For days the Lahore papers were full of the affair. As my wife recalls, an Indian who was accused turned informer and told the story of the bomb plot: The purpose was to throw the bomb into Montgomery Hall, where the European Club met, with the hope of killing many British officials. But for some reason this aim was not accomplished, perhaps on account of the brightness of the lights or the presence outside of servants and others, who would be witnesses. So the bomb was placed in the road, where it would be struck, it was hoped, by the wheel of a carriage belonging to some club member. In fact, one member starting home early on his bicycle saw the object lying in the road and was tempted to stop, but was in such a hurry that he passed by (happily for him) on the other side. It was an unfortunate Indian that received the full force of the bomb. According to the informer's account the whole plot was engineered from California, Har Dayal being the arch-conspirator. Indians were coached there by Har Dayal in the methods of violence and then sent back to India to ply their deadly trade.

About six months before the Lahore bomb outrage a similar attempt had been made at Delhi on the life of the Viceroy, Lord Hardinge. "Two Bengalis who had brought up the Delhi and Lahore bombs from Calcutta and helped to place the bomb which killed the messenger at Lahore, were convicted of the murder. One of them was sentenced to be hanged; the other, on the ground that he was the less intelligent of the two, to transportation for life. After going through the papers the Governor of the Panjab decided to ask for the death penalty on the second Bengali. After he had unsuccessfully petitioned the Viceroy for mercy and a few days before he was hanged, he informed the Criminal Investigation Officers that it was he who, disguised as a Mohammedan lady heavily veiled, and standing in front of the Panjab National Bank in the Chandni Chauk, Delhi, had thrown the bomb which killed one of the Viceroy's attendants, severely wounded the others, and caused injuries to the Viceroy which would have killed a man of less spirit and courage."[2]

"The attempt on Lord Hardinge's life was claimed by him [Har Dayal]. He invited all to help in ridding India of the British Vampire. The infamous *Ghadr* newspaper, which openly incited to murder and mutiny and urged all Indians to return to India with the express purpose of murdering the British and causing revolution by any and every means, was started by Har Dayal in 1913."[3]

It was about 1924 at the Agricultural Institute, Allahabad, that I met Nogendra Nath Sen Gupta, a member at that time of Dr. Sam Higginbottom's agricultural staff. He and his wife impressed me as cultured and charming people. I was to hear more about him later, for there appeared in *The Allahabad Pioneer* of January 9, 1925, the text of a remarkable speech by Lord Lytton, Governor of Bengal, delivered before the Bengal Council, disclosing the fact that N. Sen Gupta had been arrested in connection with the Mussalmanpara bomb case of 1914, but was acquitted of the charge of murder for lack of evidence. Later he went to England where he was a student of agriculture at Newcastle. Meanwhile he had become a Christian. When Lord Lytton visited Newcastle in 1921, he heard glowing reports from the University authorities there concerning N. Sen Gupta as "the best scholar and the finest character

[2] Sir Michael O'Dwyer, *op. cit.*, pp. 169-170.
[3] *Op. cit.*, p. 186.

that had ever come to them." Looking up the records in the India Office, Lord Lytton discovered that the agricultural student at Newcastle, England, and the accused in the bomb-throwing case of 1914 in India, were one and the same, and further, that there was strong evidence of his guilt. Coming to India the next year as Governor of Bengal, Lord Lytton found that the erstwhile bomb-thrower had sincerely repented of the crime of his youth and was determined to make amends so far as possible.

But now there was a moral question involved. N. Sen Gupta had been declared innocent by the courts, but he knew that he was guilty. It required a high standard of moral heroism to surrender the certificate of innocence given by three High Court Judges and to confess before the world his guilt. He met this supreme test of character. He not only confessed the truth to the Governor, but also gave him permission to tell before the Bengal Council the whole story, so far as it concerned himself, for in confessing his own guilt he had not in any way incriminated his former revolutionary companions.

After the Governor's published statement of January 9, 1925, which aroused wide comment and not a little misrepresentation, N. Sen Gupta followed with an open letter published in *The Statesman* of February 1, 1925. The change that had been worked in him is evident: "From my own experience I can testify that many of those engaged in terrorism are energetic young men anxious to sacrifice themselves for a noble cause. I believe, however, that a life-long sacrifice involving daily sorrowing and working for the poor, the ignorant, and the depressed millions of India demands higher character and steadier faith than a few years of secret plotting culminating in a violent and dramatic death. . . . I am convinced that the most patriotic thing I can do now is to loathe violence and to say that I loathe it."

In the same issue of *The Statesman* the following editorial comment appeared: "Mr. Sen Gupta, in our opinion, goes to the root of the matter when he suggests that the young men who are today engaged in conspiracy are such as he himself was. Far from being the dregs of society, they are as a rule recruited from amongst the most promising spirits of their generation. They come from the young men 'who see visions and who dream dreams.' "

So among the revolutionaries of India are found, as a rule, not "the dregs of society," but "the most promising spirits of their generation." We are reminded that it was a young man, Moses, the future Law-giver, who "smote the Egyptian and hid him in the sand";[4] that it was a young man, Saul of Tarsus, the future Apostle to the Gentiles, who consented to the death of Stephen and kept the garments of those that slew him.[5]

I have before me the first issue of *The Revolutionary*, January 1, 1925, which contains a Manifesto of

[4] Exodus II, 12.
[5] Acts VII, 58; XXII, 20.

the Revolutionary Party of India. It sets forth the following justification of the methods of violence.

1. Chaos and suffering are creative incidents. "Chaos is necessary to the birth of a new star, and the birth of life is accompanied by agony and pain."
2. "Foreign rule has no justification except the sword, and therefore the revolutionary party has taken to the sword. . . . Official terrorism is to be met by counter terrorism."
3. "It is a mockery to say that India's salvation can be achieved through constitutional means, since no constitution exists."
4. "Terrorism has an international bearing also, because the attention of the enemies of England is at once drawn towards India through the acts of terrorism . . . and the revolutionaries are thereby able to form an alliance with them."

Such are some of the principles set forth in this Revolutionary sheet. The aim is defined as "complete autonomy." Mr. Gandhi shares in the aim, but not in the methods of revolution. It is highly significant that the supreme personality in India today is an advocate of the methods of non-violence, as opposed to those of the revolutionaries.

"The Bhagavadgita seems to be the Hindu Scripture which has inspired both the non-violent and the violent types of agitation." [6] Mr. Gandhi, the apostle of non-violence, is reported to have spent much time during his imprisonment (1930-1931) in com-

[6] Art. on *Brahmanism and Hinduism* in *Encyclopædia of the Social Sciences*, Vol. II, p. 673-678.

menting on the Gita. The Bhagavadgita, like other sacred books, is capable of varied and contradictory interpretations. The advocates of violence, however, find proof for their policy in Gita II, 11-19, where in response to the hesitancy of Arjuna to kill his fellow men in battle, Lord Krishna reminds him of his duty as a Kshatriya to fight and kill, while at the same time comforting his heart with the philosophical assurance that even when apparently killing he does not really kill, since the spirit is not subject to death. But Mr. Gandhi says: "Swaraj depends upon our ability to control all the forces of violence on our side." It is ominous and distressing to record that on the 18th January, 1932, two Bengali school girls, neither of them over twenty years of age, went to trial in Calcutta for shooting to death Mr. C. G. B. Stevens, the District Magistrate of Comilla, Bengal.

CHAPTER XXII

MAHATMA GANDHI, INDIA'S PROPHET AND SAINT

SINCE 1920 Mohandas Karamchand Gandhi has come more and more to occupy the center of the stage in India. The title *Mahatma,* literally "great-souled," has a distinctly religious connotation. It is never applied to a mere statesman or author, but is reserved for those who by an ascetic life and advanced spiritual achievement merit that title.

Imagine a man weighing less than one hundred pounds; one who has voluntarily adopted the manner of life of almost the poorest of India's poor; like the Apostle Paul, one whose "bodily presence is weak"; in looks like Socrates who was fabled to be the ugliest man in all the Greek lands; and one by nature phenomenally shy, no orator and no great scholar in the learned tongues. Such is Mahatma Gandhi, the Statesman-Prophet of India. It is no barren claim that he has introduced religion into politics. My wife was at the Station in Saharanpur, India, in 1921, when Mr. Gandhi arrived by train. An enormous crowd was present to see his face and hear him speak. He said, "Let us stand in silent prayer." Not another word. India understood and was satisfied.

It was in South Africa, where Mr. Gandhi's income as a barrister was some £3,000 a year, that, following the example and teaching of Tolstoy, he embraced the simple life. From that time on, a modern Saint Francis, he has been wedded to poverty, making himself one with the countless poor of India and of the whole world. The description of John the Baptist's raiment–camel's hair and a leathern girdle about his loins–reminds of Mahatma Gandhi's–a loin cloth. Mr. Gandhi displays no superfluous fat–a characteristic that has helped to endear him to the Indian people, of whom the great majority are very poor. Deep spirituality in India is always associated in the thought of the people with great simplicity of life and an ascetic regimen of meats and drinks. India's traditional point of view made Mr. Gandhi especially susceptible to this aspect of Tolstoy's teaching, the ideal being furnished by India, and confirmed by Tolstoy.

Kathiawar, the region of M. K. Gandhi's birth, has produced two of the most noted personalities of modern India, Gandhi and Swami Dayanand Sarasvati, men alike marked by great independence of thought. We may perhaps trace the force of heredity. Gandhi's father was an official of the state of Porbunder, and possessed strong will and great integrity. His mother was a devout Hindu lady whose influence over her son was life-long. It was a middle-class family of the Bania or trading caste, and their type of religion was Vishnuite. Before he went to England to study law, his mother induced him to take a vow to abstain from flesh-eating, wine, and women. In his autobiography Mr. Gandhi tells with all frankness of his experiences in England and of the great blessing of the vow.

In England the youthful Gandhi began to meet Christians and to read the New Testament. He was especially impressed by the Sermon on the Mount and the Cross of Christ. He traces his doctrine of non-violence to the teaching of Christ about turning the other cheek and to the example of Christ in going to the Cross, finding it also confirmed by the noble Hindu ideal of *ahinsa.* One of his favorite hymns is "When I Survey the Wondrous Cross."

Mr. Gandhi has been several times imprisoned in India, first in 1922-1924, again in 1930, also in 1932-1933. With one voice, the people of India said during his first imprisonment that he reminded them of Christ. Mr. Gandhi thus helped to make living in India the lesson of the Cross.

One of Mr. Gandhi's great ideas is that of *satyagraha,* literally, laying hold of the truth. It is "soul-force," as opposed to bodily force. South Africa was the laboratory in which this method was perfected. It is the method of non-violent resistance against what is conceived to be injustice. It is no new thing. Every peaceful industrial strike illustrates it. So does the life of Jesus Christ and especially His submission to arrest and crucifixion. It is the method of girding up one's loins with truth rather than with a sword. In South Africa the method worked. Disabilities under which Indians had suffered were largely removed, and a new strength of character and self-respect was created in them. It involved for Mr. Gandhi and his followers stern self-discipline and self-sacrifice. More than once he was jailed, and with him hundreds of his followers. It is this inner self-discipline gained through self-sacrifice which is Mr. Gandhi's great message to India. The idea has its roots deep in religion. The saying of the wise man of Israel would doubtless appeal to Mr. Gandhi: "He that ruleth his own spirit is better than he that taketh a city."

Mr. Gandhi has always championed the cause of the outcastes of India, from the time when he accidentally touched an untouchable servant and to his mother's remonstrance replied to this effect: "How can contact with such a faithful servant defile?" Seeking to translate theory as quickly as possible into practice, he adopted a little untouchable girl into his own family. His words to India concerning the general attitude to untouchables are in substance as follows: "You have no right to home-rule, so long as you treat fellow citizens in this way. . . . If you are ill-treated by foreign nations, remember that it is a just punishment for the way you have dealt with the untouchables. If India is the pariah of the nations, it is a just nemesis for the sin of regarding a section of her own people as pariahs." [1]

This attitude toward the untouchables helps to explain Mr. Gandhi's view of caste.[2] For him caste-differences stand for division of labor, not for distinctions in dignity. In other words, caste for him means *service,* not privilege, and as thus interpreted he accepts it. It is a kind of sublimation of the doctrine of caste, or, as he would doubtless say, the explanation of caste in its original Vedic sense. It is not quite clear how Mr. Gandhi would deal with an untouchable who has the ability and spiritual insight of a Brahman.[3] At any rate, the popular theory of caste is rejected by him, and whatever one's work may be or one's ancestry may be, "A man's a man for a' that."

Mr. Gandhi refers to Untouchability under the heading, "Our Shame and Theirs." [4] It is the shame not only of India, but also of the West. For "untouchability" in India is paralleled by color distinctions in South Africa and America.[5] Thus Gandhi's

[1] See *Mahatma Gandhi's Ideas* (referred to as *M.G.I.*) by C. F. Andrews, 1930, pp. 40-41, 65, 75, 108-109, 162-179.

[2] See *M.G.I.*, p. 36. "The divisions define duties; they confer no privileges."

[3] Compare *M.G.I.*, pp. 36-37: "There is nothing to prevent the Shudra from acquiring all the knowledge he wishes. Only he will best serve with his body." Quoted with permission of the Macmillan Company, publishers

[4] See *M.G.I.*, pp. 162-179.

[5] Of this Mr. Gandhi had personal experience in South Africa, when he was debarred from a church service because of his color and race. See *M.G.I.*, pp. 176-177.

ethical survey, like that of an Old Testament prophet, is international in scope.

Mr. Gandhi accepts Transmigration as a doctrine of Hinduism. In harmony therewith he longs for final release, but so long as that is impossible, expresses the wish to be born as an untouchable, in order to be fully identified with that section of the people of India most in need of sympathy and help. Thus even the theory of transmigration yields in his hands a program of selfless service. The dauntless spirit of Gandhi is prepared again and again to become flesh, if only thereby he can serve.

Mahatma Gandhi has had an international experience, having lived in India, England, and South Africa. Hence his international mind, which furnishes the best background for a true nationalism.

The idea of *Swadeshi* is fundamental in Gandhi's thinking. It means devotion to one's own country, that is to say, nationalism. In a Kantian sense he has universalized the notion, and so regards it as the duty and privilege of every nation, nay, of every natural group. It means provision for one's own, and Mr. Gandhi would doubtless accept whole-heartedly the saying, "If any provideth not for his own, he hath denied the faith, and is worse than an infidel." [6] *Swadeshi* has several aspects. There is political *swadeshi*. It is, in Woodrow Wilson's phrase, "the right of self-determination." It is the right to cherish one's own political institutions, the right to self-

[6] 1 Timothy, V, 8.

government. India has this right, because every nation has it. There is economic *swadeshi,* the protection and development of one's own natural industries. The boycotting of foreign cloth, the use of *khaddar,* and the cult of the spinning wheel all belong under this head. There is religious *swadeshi,* adherence to, and purification of, the religious traditions of one's own country. Mr. Gandhi calls himself an "orthodox Hindu," [7] but he also says, "If 'untouchability' belongs to the Hindu religion, then I am not a Hindu." [8] Which means that Mr. Gandhi purposes to reform Hinduism and lift it to his ideal of what it ought to be. For this reason he denounces "untouchability," exploitation of the poor, drunkenness, and addiction to drugs, and prostitution, both secular and religious. Gandhi's position is that all religions, if reformed and taken seriously, contain sufficient truth to produce character. Hence, in his opinion, proselytism is always and everywhere a mistake, and should be replaced by philanthropy, the expression of one's religious convictions in the form of deeds alone. There is also educational *swadeshi,* the development of one's own language and methods of culture. National schools in India are the outcome of this idea and also the growing emphasis on the cultivation of the vernaculars.

Another great principle of Mr. Gandhi is *ahinsa* (non-killing, or non-violence). There is a famous passage in the Great Epic: "*Ahinsa* is the supreme

[7] *M.G.I.*, p. 166. [8] *M.G.I.*, p. 65.

piety." This idea lies at the basis of that reverence for all life which characterizes India. Mr. Gandhi translates *ahinsa* by "love," thereby making the idea positive. It is a spirit or temper like the love that "suffereth long and is kind" (1 Cor. XIII, 4). And it is to be rationally applied, not in the letter, but in the spirit. Accordingly, we see Mr. Gandhi agreeing to put a severely wounded calf out of its misery by the administration of an opiate poison, thereby scandalizing the extreme conservatives. Under the circumstances it was a manifestation of *ahinsa*. The implications of this interpretation are frankly faced by Mr. Gandhi, and so he admits that there might conceivably be circumstances when a similar method would be justified in the case of human beings. In other words, mere non-killing is not *ahinsa*. True *ahinsa* is "love."

Great teachers have ever had the habit of organizing schools or retreats for the training of disciples, and also to serve as the centers of propaganda. Such is Rabindranath Tagore's school at Shantiniketan and Mr. Gandhi's *ashram* at Sabarmati (now closed). Gandhi's *ashram* was intended as a kind of laboratory or power-house for the creation of soul-force. It was like a mediæval monastery in the strictness of its discipline. Those admitted subscribed to a series of vows: truth at any cost; *ahinsa,* life-long celibacy, control of the palate, non-thieving, non-possession of things not needful, *swadeshi,* fearlessness, justice to the untouchables, education in the vernacular, the vow of *khaddar,* and the religious use of politics.

M. K. Gandhi professes to be an orthodox Hindu, but, as has been shown, he gives his own interpretation to the essential things of Hinduism. The Hindu scriptures are accepted for "substance of doctrine," but not in detail. Caste is regarded, in its original Vedic form of the four orders, as rooted in human nature, and as indicative of duty, not of privilege. Cow-protection is taken as a symbol of the kindness due to all sub-human creatures. The use of images in worship is admitted, whenever it is found helpful in devotion, that is to say, Mr. Gandhi does not "disbelieve in idol worship." Numerous *avataras,* or "incarnations" [9] of the divine, are vouched for by the Hindu scriptures, and so are accepted according to a famous verse of the Gita. In harmony therewith Christ is regarded as one among many, "a radiant revelation of God, but not the only revelation." Transmigration is accepted apparently in its full orthodox sense. It is the old Hinduism to some extent revised and prophetically interpreted by a man of singular ethical temper. Gandhi has sought to do for modern Hinduism what Amos, Hosea, Isaiah and Jeremiah sought to do for old Hebraism, namely, to raise on the old foundations a structure nearer the ideal. His criticism of the religious practices of Hinduism is tempered throughout by his affection for Hinduism as a whole. "I know that vice is going on today in all the great Hindu shrines, but I love

[9] See *M.G.I.,* p. 35.

them in spite of their unspeakable failings. . . . I am a reformer through and through, but my zeal never leads me to the rejection of any of the essential things of Hinduism." [10]

Mr. Gandhi believes in God, in prayer, in the centrality of the ethical, in the sacredness of human personality, and is thus linked up with devout theists of every religion. In fact, there are five virtues in M. K. Gandhi worthy of mention: devotion to the poor, reliance on love, sacrificial spirit, trust in God, prayerful life.

Patriotism has been at different times conceived practically as a religion. Japan, Soviet Russia, old China, and the Roman Empire with its cult of the Emperor, all illustrate the religion of patriotism. For M. K. Gandhi *Swaraj,* or self-rule, has the centrality of a fundamental religious principle. His "five points" of *swaraj* are the use of *khaddar,* that is, economic independence, Hindu-Muslim unity, removal of untouchability, equality of women, prohibition of the liquor traffic, five points, like the five fingers, bound into a unity by the principle of non-violence. Here Mr. Gandhi appears as a religious statesman interested in nation-building. From all other nation-builders, however, he differs because of his profound belief in non-violence.

Mr. Gandhi's theism is described by Dr. N. Macnicol as "agnostic," apparently on the ground that

[10] *M.G.I.*, p. 40. Quoted with permission of the Macmillan Company.

Mr. Gandhi is unwilling to propagate it by word of mouth, it being ill-defined in his own mind. His principle is "Live your religion and let the living do the preaching." He would doubtless accept the idea set forth in the second part of Chaucer's famous couplet:

> But Christes lore and His Apostles twelve
> He taught, *but first he followed it himselve.*

This emphasis on doing as contrasted with speaking is in general sound. Only it must be remembered that, if doing is a form of saying, saying also is a form of doing. Mr. Gandhi's theism is able to inspire in him the attitude of trust and devotion toward God, and to give him the spirit of helpfulness toward the poor and downtrodden, and capacity for love and self-sacrifice. It has made him the supreme ethical voice in contemporary Hinduism. Judged by its results, it is a living faith. His principle that all religions are true also by necessary implication prevents for him the propaganda of any particular form of religion, except that by the principle of *swaraj* he naturally champions Hinduism for the Hindus.

One of the most "revealing" [11] acts in Mr. Gandhi's life was the "Great Fast." It followed hard on the operation for appendicitis at the close of his two years' imprisonment (1922-1924). Hindus and Musalmans had broken out into communal strife, which had reached its climax in the horrors of Kohat.

[11] See *M.G.I.*, pp. 302-318.

Days and nights were spent by Mr. Gandhi in vigil and prayer, seeking for divine guidance. The result was a fast of twenty-one days as a penitential act [12] because of the sins of his own people. It was in a very real sense vicarious, the innocent suffering on behalf of the guilty. It was so understood, the news of it filling the masses with awe, so that immediately the riots ceased. On the twelfth day of the fast his life seemed to be in danger, and he was urged to take food. His reply was: "Have faith in God. . . . You have forgotten the power of prayer." [13] In spite of weakness of body the fast was completed, and a favorite hymn was sung: "The way to God is only meant for heroes; it is not meant for cowards." A little later Mr. Andrews was asked to sing, "When I Survey the Wondrous Cross." [14]

While the fast was going on, representative Hindus, Muhammadans and Christians [15] were in conference near by, seeking to promote a better mutual understanding. "The problem of Hindu-Muslim unity has thus been carried a long way farther towards solution by Mahatma Gandhi's heroic act of faith." [16]

[12] Explained by Mr. Gandhi, however, as "for his own self-purification," *op. cit.*, p. 303.

[13] *Op. cit.*, p. 304. "No act of mine is done without prayer" is Mr. Gandhi's testimony. If a certain foreign missionary deserves the title "Praying Hyde," no less does the Indian statesman deserve the title "Praying Gandhi."

[14] *M.G.I.*, pp. 308, 315.

[15] The Metropolitan of India, C. F. Andrews, and Dr. S. K. Datta were the Christians present.

[16] C. F. Andrews, *M.G.I.*, p. 318.

As we have seen, Mr. Gandhi seeks to explain the various metaphysical positions of Hinduism in such a way as to yield nutriment for the moral life. Take for example, his comment on the great Vedanta text, "One only without a second." "I believe," said he, "in the absolute oneness of God, and therefore of humanity. What though we have bodies? We have but one soul. . . . I cannot therefore detach myself from the wickedest soul, nor may I be denied identity with the most virtuous." [17] This sounds like the absolute non-dualism of Shankara.

As is inevitable in the case of the greatest characters of history, Mr. Gandhi has been the object of considerable criticism. "Why," asked many of his admirers both in India and abroad, "did Mr. Gandhi not patiently and hopefully await the first Round Table Conference, instead of precipitously launching a program of non-violent violence?" The result was his own imprisonment together with that of some thirty thousand of his followers, and the prevention of the Nationalists taking part in the first London Conference. This much is to be said, however: that the salt-raids and the picketing of foreign cloth and of Indian liquor shops have revealed to Britain and to the world the growing strength of India's determination for a position of national self-respect and her preparedness for self-sacrifice on behalf of it. Or take the matter of caste. Here Gandhi and Tagore

[17] *M.G.I.*, p. 305. Quoted with permission of the Macmillan Company, publishers.

represent somewhat different points of view. The fundamentalists of Hinduism were shocked at Gandhi's new interpretation of *ahinsa,* as illustrated in his treatment of the wounded calf. Mr. C. F. Andrews, too, has not seen eye to eye with Mr. Gandhi in the matter of the encouragement of recruiting for the world war, the burning of foreign cloth, and the vow of life-long celibacy.[18]

Mr. Gandhi once apparently considered seriously the matter of becoming a Christian.[19] But he has remained a Hindu, finding his religious nutriment in the Bhagavadgita and Upanishads and next to them in the Gospel of Christ, especially the Sermon on the Mount and the Cross.[20] A gleam from the Cross of Christ has thus lighted up Mr. Gandhi's pathway. Christendom should be thankful that Mr. Gandhi has followed the "gleam" as faithfully as he has. Let those who are tempted to take up stones of criticism refrain until they have been as faithful to the highest they know as M. K. Gandhi has been to the highest he knows.

These are all the fair and honest criticisms of friends, but there are also objections of another type. For example, that of an editor, who declares that "Gandhiji, the supposed friend of Musalmans, has as his real aim in uplifting the untouchables, to make them into powerful and fiery soldiers of the Hindus."

[18] Especially Mr. Gandhi's conception of marriage as a "fall." *M.G.I.,* pp. 37, 42.

[19] *Mahatma Gandhi* by Gray and Parekh, 1924, pp. 10, 104.

[20] *M.G.I.,* p. 73.

An editorial in *The C. & M. Gazette*, Lahore, declares also, that "a dictatorship alone would satisfy him" (Mr. Gandhi), a kind of admission that M. K. Gandhi is actually the uncrowned king of India today. As *The Nation* (September 30, 1931) puts it, we have in the second Round Table Conference the spectacle of "one naked little man . . . negotiating with the British Empire."

Mr. Gandhi, like other men, can make mistakes. Such was his assurance to India in 1921 that *swaraj* would be gained immediately, and also his ultimatum to the Government that *swaraj* must be given to India by January 1, 1930. But Britain too, in the opinion of many, has made mistakes; witness the Rowlatt legislation, the appointment of Lord Birkenhead as Secretary of State for India, and the Simon Commission with no Indian representatives on it.

Some estimates of Mahatma Gandhi will indicate how he impresses different people. Romain Rolland, the French savant, refers to M. K. Gandhi as "the man who became one with the Universal Being." Reverend Mr. Holmes regards him as "not only incomparably the greatest man in the world today, but one of the ten or dozen greatest men who have ever lived." And similarly Kirby Page: "More than any other man of the age the spinner of Sabarmati reminds me of the Carpenter of Nazareth." An Anglican Bishop writes: "He appeals to the hearts of the Indian people as no other man has done, probably since the days of Buddha." Dr. Stanley Jones refers to Gandhi as "actually living the sermon of Christ on the Mount." And C. F. Andrews, so long and intimately associated with Mahatma Gandhi, says of him: "He is most nearly of any one I know the St. Francis of the modern age, the Little Brother of the Poor." A people that can produce a character like Gandhi is not effete, and will be heard from further.

CHAPTER XXIII

RABINDRANATH TAGORE AND "THE RELIGION OF MAN"

BORN of an illustrious Brahman family of Bengal, at home in the thought of both the East and the West, poet, dramatist, novelist and winner of the Nobel prize for literature, founder of the Bolpur school at Shantiniketan, and dreamer of the establishment in India of a World University, Rabindranath Tagore is citizen of India and citizen of the world. The sage of Bolpur and the statesman-saint, M. K. Gandhi, represent the flower of present-day Hindu achievement in the way of creative personalities.

Rabindranath was born May 6, 1861, son of Debendranath Tagore, the famous Brahmo leader. His father was austere and his mother died when he was a child. He disliked tutors and escaped school, because, as he tells us, he "felt like a caged rabbit in a biological institute."[1] His own home furnished him amply with cultural materials and cultural interests, music, literature, art; and besides there was the world of nature to explore. His father took him on a visit to the Himalayas; and the Ganges at his very door, now flowing placidly, now rough with

[1] *Religion of Man*, p. 97.

wind and flood, was a part of his very life. In fact, he was a "river-poet" first and last. Thus Rabindranath's real education came from "the whole circumstances and environment of his life" [2] rather than from formal study at school. It was in the light of these early experiences that the sage of Bolpur at the age of forty began his notable educational experiment at Shantiniketan, in which he sought to develop in the children of his school "the feeling of intimacy with nature" which marked the first stage in his own religious experience. It was a modern adaptation of the forest-schools of ancient India.

By inheritance and early training Rabindranath Tagore was a Brahmo. He tells us how in his youth he received from his father a secretarial post and composed hymns for the theistic worship, but that finally he discovered that his loyalty was to a "religious institution" rather than to "religion" itself. So "after a long struggle," he writes, "I gave up my connection with our church," having the feeling that "that which is common to a group is not important." [3] Thompson, however, is undoubtedly right in saying that Rabindranath "is unmistakably Brahmo, in his strong clear theism and his insistence on personal relationship with God as the thing that matters." [4] So, while Rabindranath Tagore holds essentially the theistic position of the Brahmo Samaj,

[2] Thompson, *Rabindranath Tagore*, p. 7.
[3] *Religion of Man*, pp. 107-108.
[4] *Rabindranath Tagore*, p. 105.

it seems that he has, institutionally at least, reverted to Hinduism. His action in the matter has doubtless encouraged many who might otherwise have become Brahmos, to stay within the society of Hinduism and be known as Hindus, while at the same time cherishing Brahmo convictions concerning God and duty. Is this one reason why the Brahmo Samaj is growing in numbers so slowly, because many Brahmos, like many undeclared Christians, still remain within the capacious fold of Hinduism?

Rabindranath distinguishes between second-hand religion—that of mere tradition—and the first-hand religion of personal experience. Two creative moments came to him in his boyhood and young manhood, that time of life when, according to Wordsworth, one is specially sensitive to the intimations of the unseen world. "When I was eighteen," he writes, "a sudden spring breeze of religious experience for the first time came to my life and passed away leaving in my memory a direct message of spiritual reality. One day while I stood watching at early dawn the sun sending out its rays from behind the trees, I suddenly felt as if some ancient mist had in a moment lifted from my sight, and the morning light on the face of the world revealed an inner radiance of joy. The invisible screen of the commonplace was removed from all things and all men and their ultimate significance" were laid bare.[5] This state of mys-

[5] From Rabindranath Tagore, *The Religion of Man*, pp. 91-92. By permission of the Macmillan Company, publishers.

tical consciousness, which had its origin in the apocalypse at early dawn, lasted four days.[6]

There was a later experience of the same sort, when Rabindranath one morning, after his work was over, was looking out of his window at a very ordinary scene, that of "a dry river bed welcoming the first flood of rain along its channel." Then a sudden consciousness of "a stirring of soul." "Facts that were detached and dim found a great unity of meaning." It was as if "a man groping through a fog . . . suddenly discovers that he stands before his own house." [7]

Thus Rabindranath's religion is that of a poet, the sources of his religious inspiration lying close to those of his poetic inspiration.[8] The two apocalyptic moments of insight were the occasion of poems, *The Awakening of the Waterfall* and *The Lord of My Life*. Let me quote from the latter:

> I see thine eyes gazing at the dark of my heart.
> Lord of my life,
> I wonder if my failures and wrongs are forgiven.
> For many were my days without service
> and nights of forgetfulness;
> futile were the flowers that faded in the shade
> not offered to thee.
> Often the tired strings of my lute
> slackened at the strain of thy tunes.

[6] I recall a similar state of mystical consciousness in my boyhood, which also lasted three or four days.

[7] *Religion of Man*, p. 93.

[8] It is not without significance that such a large part of the world's religious literature is poetry.

And often at the ruin of wasted hours
my desolate evenings were filled with tears.[9]

Such experience enshrined in poetry was gained not through striving, but through what Wordsworth calls "a wise passiveness." Rabindranath, as Walt Whitman would say, was loafing and inviting his soul, when "an unexpected train of thoughts ran across his mind like a strange caravan carrying the wealth of an unknown kingdom." [10]

As regards the religious fruitage of these early experiences, the poet has gained a first-hand realization of the difference between "the obscurity of an ordinary fact" as seen through the ordinary consciousness, and its "ultimate significance" as grasped by the heightened and mystical consciousness, the morning light on the face of the world revealing to the latter "an inner radiance of joy," and facts that were detached and dim finding "a great unity of meaning." Thus, as it were, "the invisible screen of the commonplace was removed," and there was given "a direct message of spiritual reality." [11]

The book which describes these experiences and their implications is Rabindranath's *Religion of Man*. These lectures gather up and present in a more or less consistent and formal manner the occasional statements concerning religion found in his

[9] From Rabindranath Tagore, *The Religion of Man*, p. 96. By permission of the Macmillan Company, publishers.
[10] *Op. cit.*, p. 96.
[11] *Op. cit.*, pp. 92-94.

earlier works; hence a kind of biographical summary of his religious experiences and convictions. Rabindranath, as he asserts, is neither a philosopher nor a theologian, but a poet. *The Religion of Man* is a kind of prose-poem marked by the suggestiveness and also by the elusiveness of great poetry. The book required three readings before I felt sure that I even measurably grasped its thought.

The poet begins on the level of ordinary experience with man individual and particular, different from all other individuals. Even in his concrete individuality and imperfection man is declared to be at once the best expression of the universe and the best representative of the Infinite Spirit, God.[12] But the individual man implies "the general idea of man," as the imperfect copy implied for Plato the perfect idea. This perfect idea is declared to be "the infinite ideal of Man," the "divine Humanity," the "ideal of father, friend and beloved," "the Eternal Person"—at once infinite and finite—"manifested in all persons."[13]

We note the poet's conviction of the truth of personality. "Religions are never about a God of cosmic force, but rather about the God of human personality," the "Supreme Person, whose Spirit is over us all," "the Person, who is in the heart of all."[14] In several places he deals with the impersonal state

[12] Compare man made in the image of God. Genesis I, 27.
[13] *Religion of Man*, p. 163.
[14] *Op. cit.*, pp. 17, 22, 113.

sought by the Yogi as contrasted with the personal consciousness. While admitting that the first "may be valuable as a great psychological experience," and as such cannot logically be refuted, he declares that "it is not religion," since religion requires the dualism of the Infinite Spirit and finite spirits, so that "the bond of devotion with God may continue for ever." Religion is not instrumental to the attainment of an impersonal state beyond itself, but is "ultimate." [15] In thus refusing to regard the impersonal as a higher category than the personal, Rabindranath definitely associates himself with Ramanuja, rather than with Shankara.

The ethical nature of man is rooted in a kind of double consciousness, the consciousness of individuality and of all the desires and activities that go with the narrowly circumscribed self, and also the consciousness of something transcendental, the higher Self, the Over Soul, the Supreme Man, which is immanent in all as "the Infinite Ideal of Man," making us aware of the unattained which we *ought* to attain, for there is an instinct which prompts to the quest of the "Endless Further." [16] Or, differently stated, "on the surface of our being we have the everchanging phases of the individual self, but in the depth there dwells the Eternal Spirit," who "invokes unexpectedly in the midst of a self-centered life a supreme sacrifice," at whose call we "dedicate our lives to the

[15] *Op. cit.*, pp. 115, 200-201, 203-204.
[16] *Op. cit.*, p. 202.

cause of truth and beauty."[17] Such self-dedication or renunciation of the lower self at the summons of the Higher is "the chief end of man." Religion consists in faith in the Supreme Spirit and in the endeavor to express those qualities that are inherent in Him. Thus ethics means the bringing of the lower self into harmony with the Higher Self. Failure to accomplish this harmony is sin.

Duty is summed up in love, for "the Infinite One is infinite Love." "The Supreme One, who relates all things, comprehends the universe, is all love—the love that is the highest truth being the most perfect relationship." Love is ultimate and an eternal bond between the infinite and the finite soul.[18] Man is imprisoned in the bondage of his limited self, and only attains freedom when liberated in the Infinite Self, not the liberation of absorption or identity as Shankara taught, but the liberty of union and communion with God through love for Him and love for fellow men.

The end of love is unity among men. This unity has its metaphysical ground and pledge of possibility in the fact that the Infinite Spirit is immanent in all men as "love" and so is "the Eternal Spirit of human unity." The consciousness of this unity is something spiritual, and "our effort to be true to it is our religion."[19] In the light of these great convictions

[17] *Op. cit.*, pp. 15-16, 179-180.
[18] *Op cit.*, pp. 64, 98, 188.
[19] *Op. cit.*, p. 14.

Rabindranath "refuses to think that the twin spirits of the East and the West, the Mary and Martha, can never meet to make perfect the realization of truth." [20]

Mystical experience may help to solve a subjective conflict between the familiar old and the questionable but fascinating new, as in the examples of St. Paul and Sadhu Sundar Singh. But usually it simply strengthens beliefs already held, but held with too little vividness and conviction, by furnishing them with an experiential basis. Examples of this are Isaiah, the Old Testament prophet, and Rabindranath Tagore. The mystical experiences of the latter simply furnished him with stronger foundations for the Brahmo attitudes and convictions already cherished by him. If Isaiah's vision was clothed in the imagery of the Temple, Rabindranath's apocalypse was received through the phenomena of nature, the essential thing in both experiences being inner illumination. Isaiah was impressed by the majesty of God and with a sense that he was a man of "unclean lips." [21] In Rabindranath's commemorative poem, *Jivan Devata* (The Lord of My Life), one of the notes struck is the penitential note, the poet wondering if his "failures and wrongs are forgiven," often "at the ruin of wasted hours" filling his desolate evenings "with tears." But in both instances "numinous" and

[20] *Op. cit.*, p. 176.
[21] Isaiah VI, 5.

mystical experience was the root which bore fruit in the form of a wide ministry, Isaiah, the prophet, leaving to the world the book called by his name, and Rabindranath Tagore speaking to his generation in *The Religion of Man.*

BIBLIOGRAPHY

CHAPTERS I AND II

Crooke, W., *Popular Religion of Northern India.*

—— "Hinduism," *Encyclopedia of Religion and Ethics* (E.R.E.).

Das, G., *Hinduism,* Madras, Natesan and Co., 1924.

—— *Hindu Ethics,* Madras, Natesan and Co., 1927.

Eliot, Sir Charles, *Hinduism and Buddhism,* London, Arnold, 1921, 3 vols.

Farquhar, J. N., *Primer of Hinduism,* London, Oxford University Press, 2nd ed., 1912.

—— *The Crown of Hinduism.*

Griswold, H. D., *Religion of the Rigveda,* London, Oxford University Press, 1923.

—— "Indian Pessimism," E.R.E.

—— "Brahmanism and Hinduism," *Encyclopædia of the Social Sciences,* N. Y., Macmillan, 1930.

Hillebrandt, A., *Vedische Mythologie.*

Hume, R. E., *World's Living Religions.*

Keith, A. B., *The Religion and Philosophy of the Vedas and Upanishads,* Harvard University Press, 1925, 2 vols.

Ketkar, S. V., *Essay on Hinduism.*

Lyall, Sir Alfred, *Asiatic Studies.*

MacDonell, A. A., *A History of Sanskrit Literature.*

Monier-Williams, Sir Monier, *Brahmanism and Hinduism,* N. Y., Macmillan, 1891.

Müller, F. M., *Physical Religion.*

Oldenberg, H., *Die Religion des Veda.*

Risley, H., *Census of India,* 1901.
Sen, G. P., *Census of India,* 1901.
Shilotri, P. S., *Indo-Aryan Thought and Culture,* 1913.
Vidyarnava, S. C., *A Catechism of Hindu Dharma,* 1919.

CHAPTER III

Appasamy, A. J., *Christianity as Bhakti Marga,* Madras, C. L. S., 1926 (Introduction).
Griswold, H. D., *Brahman: A Study in the History of Indian Philosophy,* N. Y., Macmillan, 1900.
Farquhar, J. N., *An Outline of the Religious Literature of India,* London, Oxford University Press, 1920 (Chapters III and VI).
Macnicol, Nicol, *Indian Theism,* London, Oxford University Press, 1915.
Otto, Rudolf, *India's Religion of Grace and Christianity,* Eng. trans., Frank Hugh Foster, London, Student Christian Movement Press, 1930.
— *The Idea of the Holy,* Eng. trans., John W. Harvey, London, Oxford University Press, 1925.
Radhakrishnan, S., *Indian Philosophy,* N. Y., Macmillan, 1923, Vol. I (Introduction).
Thibaut, Prof., S. B. E., XXXIV.

CHAPTER IV

Farquhar, J. N., Art., "Brahma Samaj," *Encyclopedia of Religion and Ethics.*
Mozoomdar, P. C., *The Oriental Christ,* Calcutta.
Sen, Keshab Chander, *Lectures in India.*
Sastri, Sivanath, *History of the Brahmo Samaj,* Calcutta, Chatterji, 1911-1912, 2 vols.
Smith, George, *Life of Alexander Duff.*

CHAPTER V

Farquhar, J. N., *Modern Religious Movements in India,* N. Y., Macmillan, 1915.

Gupta, N., Art., "Ramakrishna Paramhansa," *Modern Review,* Calcutta, May-June, 1928.

MacDonell, A. A., "Ramakrishna," E.R.E., X.

Madhavananda, Swami, ed., *The Life of Sri Ramakrishna,* Almora (India), Advaita Ashrama, 1925.

Müller, F. M., *Ramakrishna: His Life and Sayings,* N. Y., 1899.

Rolland, Romain, Art., "Ramakrishna—A Modern Avatar," *Asia,* N. Y., 1929-1930.

Thomas, Wendell, *Hinduism Invades America,* N. Y., Beacon, 1930.

CHAPTER VI

Barrows, J. H., ed., *The World's Parliament of Religions,* 1893, 2 vols.

Farquhar, J. N., *Modern Religious Movements in India,* N. Y., Macmillan, 1915.

Thomas, Wendell, *Hinduism Invades America,* N. Y., Beacon, 1930.

Virajananda, Swami, ed., *Life of Swami Vivekananda,* Almora (India), Advaita Ashrama, 1924-1928.

Vivekananda, Swami, *Complete Works,* Almora (India), 1919-1922, 7 vols., Mayavati Memorial Edition.

CHAPTER VII

Singh, Puran, *The Story of Swami Ram Tirath, the Poet-Monk of the Punjab,* Madras, Ganesh, 1924.

Tirath, Swami Ram, *Complete Works,* under the title *In*

the Woods of God-Realization, Lucknow (India), 1930-1931, 3 vols.

CHAPTER VIII

Bechofer-Roberts, C. E., *The Mysterious Madam,* N. Y., 1931.

Besant, Mrs. A., *Is Theosophy Anti-Christian?,* 1904.

Cleather, Alice L., *H. P. Blavatsky: A Great Betrayal,* Calcutta, 1922.

Farquhar, J. N., *Modern Religious Movements in India,* N. Y., Macmillan, 1915, pp. 208-291.

Kuhn, A. B., *Theosophy, A Modern Revival of Ancient Wisdom,* N. Y., Henry Holt, 1930.

Krishnamurti, Jiddu, Pamphlets:—

1. *The Poet of Wisdom,* including *Who Brings the Truth?, By What Authority?* and *Three Poems,* 1928.
2. *Life the Goal,* 1928.
3. *Let Understanding be the Law.*
4. *Life and Conduct* in *A Free Pulpit in Action,* 1931, pp. 261-269.

Olcott, Col. H. S., *Old Diary Leaves,* 1927.

Solovyoff, V. S., *A Modern Priestess of Isis,* London, Longmans, 1895. Eng. trans. by Walter Leaf. (Out of print.)

"Veritas," *Mrs. Besant and the Alcyone Case,* Madras, Goodwin, 1913.

Witte, Count, *Memoirs,* 1921, pp. 4-10.

——*Proceedings of the British Society of Psychic Research,* London, Trubner, IX, pp. 201-400 (1885); XXIV, pp. 129-159 (1893).

——"Madam Blavatsky," *Dictionary of American Biography,* 1929, Vol. II, pp. 361-363.

CHAPTER IX

Griswold, H. D., *Pandit Agnihotri and the Deva Samaj,* in Report of the North India Conference of Christian Workers, 1903. (Out of print.)

Farquhar, J. N., *Modern Religious Movements in India,* N. Y., Macmillan, 1915, pp. 173-182.

Agnihotri, S. N., editor-in-chief, *Science-Grounded Religion,* Lahore (India), 1905-1927, Vols. I-XXII.

—— Pamphlets, especially:

1. *The Advent of a Science-Grounded Religion for all Mankind,* 1913.
2. *Who is the Deva Atma and why do we Worship him?,* 1917.
3. *God-belief and its Horrible Results,* 1921.
4. *All about the Dev Samaj,* 1923.
5. *Forty Years Work of the Dev Samaj,* 1924.

CHAPTER X

Agnihotri, S. N., *Pandit Dayanand Unveiled,* 1891. (Out of print.)

Durga Prasad, *An English Translation of the Satyarth Prakash,* Lahore, Virjanand Press, 1908.

Farquhar, J. N., *Modern Religious Movements in India,* N. Y., Macmillan, 1915.

Griswold, H. D., "The Problem of the Arya Samaj," *Indian Evangelical Review, Calcutta,* 1902.

—— *Dayanandi Interpretation of the Word "Deva" in the Rigveda,* Ludhiana (India), 1897. (Out of print.)

—— "Arya Samaj," E.R.E., 1910.

—— *Religion of the Rigveda,* London, Oxford University Press, 1923.

Oman, J. C., *Cults, Customs and Superstitions of India,* 1908, Chapter VII.

Dayananda, Swami, *Theosophist,* Oct. and Dec., 1879, and Nov., 1880, fragment of an autobiography of Swami Dayanand.

Singh, Chhajja, *The Life and Teachings of Swami Dayanand Saraswati,* Lahore, Addison Press, 1903, 2 vols.

CHAPTER XI

Griswold, H. D., *The Radha Swami Sect,* Cawnpore (India), Christ Church Mission Press, 1908. (Out of print.)

—— *Radha Swami Sect,* Nur Afshan newspaper (Urdu), Ludhiana, India, Oct. 14, 1898.

Farquhar, J. N., *Modern Religious Movements in India,* N. Y., 1915, pp. 157-173.

—— "Radha Soamis," *Encyclopedia of Religion and Ethics,* 1919, Vol. X, pp. 558-559.

—— *Dayal Bagh,* A Brief Account of the Radha Soami Satsang, 1928. For other literature of the Radha Soamis see footnotes.

CHAPTER XII

Farquhar, J. N., *Outline of the Religious Literature of India,* London, Oxford University Press, 1920.

Jacobi, H., trans., *Sacred Books of the East,* Vol. XXII.

Jaini, Jagmanderlal, *Outlines of Jainism,* 1916.

Stevenson, Mrs. Sinclair, *The Heart of Jainism,* London, Oxford University Press, 1915.

CHAPTER XIII

Griswold, H. D., *The Chet Rami Sect,* Cawnpore, Christ Church Mission Press, 1904. (Out of print.)

Farquhar, J. N., *Modern Religious Movements in India*, N. Y., Macmillan, 1915, pp. 150-156.

Talib-ud-Din, Rev., Article in *Nur Afshan* (in Urdu), Ludhiana (India), May 23, 1889.

—— *Lodiana Mission Reports*, 1879, pp. 22-26; 1888, pp. 10-11.

—— *Census of India*, 1881 (Vol. I, p. 287); 1891; 1901 (Vol. XVII, p. 117).

CHAPTER XIV

Heiler, Friedrich, *Sadhu Sundar Singh Ein Apostel des Ostens und Westens*, München, 1926.

Otto, Rudolf, *The Idea of the Holy*, London, 1925.

Streeter, B. H., and Appasamy, A. J., *The Sadhu, A Study in Mysticism and Practical Religion.*

CHAPTER XV

Farquhar, J. N., *Outline of the Religious Literature of India.*

Stevenson, Mrs. Sinclair, *The Heart of Jainism*, London, Oxford University Press, 1915 (under Digambara).

CHAPTER XVI

Dyer, Helen S., *Pandita Ramabai: The Story of Her Life*, 1900.

Macnicol, Nicol, *Pandita Ramabai*, Calcutta, Association Press, 1926.

Ramabai Sarasvati, Pandita, *The High Caste Hindu Woman*, 1887.

CHAPTER XVII

See books mentioned in footnotes.

CHAPTER XVIII

Crooke, W., "Bhangi," *Encyclopedia of Religion and Ethics,* 1910, Vol. II, pp. 551-553.

Griswold, H. D., "Bhangi Priesthood, Altar and Sacrifice," *Indian Witness,* Lucknow, India, July 20, 27 and Aug. 3, 1921.

—— "Ecstasy, Spirit-possession and Exorcism among the Bhangis," *Indian Witness,* Aug. 10 and 17, 1921.

CHAPTER XIX

Griswold, H. D., "The Chuhra Jag," *Indian Standard.*

Strickler, H. J., *The Religion and Customs of the Chuhra in the Punjab Province, India* (M. A. Dissertation in MS.), 1926.

Youngson, Dr., "Chuhra," *Encyclopedia of Religion and Ethics.*

—— *Indian Antiquary,* Vols. XXXV-XXXVI, 1906-1907.

CHAPTER XX

Farquhar, J. N., *Outline of the Religious Literature of India,* London, Oxford University Press, 1920 (Chap. VII, *Muslim Influence,* pp. 284-361).

Titus, M. T., *Indian Islam,* London, Oxford University Press, 1929.

CHAPTER XXI

O'Dwyer, Sir Michael, *India as I Knew It, 1885-1925,* 1925.

Lord Lytton, "Terrorism in Bengal," *Pioneer,* Allahabad, Jan. 9, 1925.

Gupta, N. Sen, Open Letter in the *Statesman*, Calcutta, Feb. 1, 1925.

—— Editorial on "Terrorism," *Statesman*, Calcutta, Feb. 1, 1925.

CHAPTER XXII

Andrews, C. F., ed., *Mahatma Gandhi's Ideas*, N. Y., Macmillan, 1930.

—— ed., *Mahatma Gandhi–His Own Story*, N. Y., Macmillan, 1930.

—— ed., *Mahatma Gandhi at Work*, 1931.

Gandhi, M. K., *Freedom's Battle*, Madras, Ganesh, 1921.

—— *Experiments with Truth.*

Gray, R. M., and Parekh, M. C., *Mahatma Gandhi, An Essay in Appreciation*, Calcutta, Association Press, 1924.

CHAPTER XXIII

Tagore, Rabindranath, *The Religion of Man*, N. Y., Macmillan, 1931 (Hibbert Lectures for 1930).

Thompson, E. J., *Rabindranath Tagore.*

INDEX